Wilton's Music Hall
and
Hero Productions
present

The Box of Delights

by Piers Torday

based on the novel by
John Masefield

First performed at Wilton's Music Hall on 1 December, 2017
A Wilton's Music Hall and Hero Productions Commission

The Company

Mark Extance	**The Bishop of Tatchester and Train Conductor**
Josefina Gabrielle	**Sylvia Daisy Pouncer and Caroline Louisa**
Safiyya Ingar	**Maria Jones**
Tom Kanji	**Charles and the Inspector of Police**
Matthew Kelly	**Cole Hawlings and Abner Brown**
Samuel Simmonds	**Peter Jones**
Rosalind Steele	**Herne the Hunter, Rat and Abner's Head**
Alistair Toovey	**Kay Harker**

Creative Team

Piers Torday	**Writer**
Justin Audibert	**Director**
Tom Piper	**Designer**
Anna Watson	**Lighting Designer**
Ed Lewis	**Composer and Sound Designer**
Nina Dunn	**Video Designer**
Simon Pittman	**Movement Director**
Samuel Wyer	**Puppetry Designer**
Vicky Richardson	**Casting Director**

Production Team

Cath Bates	**Production Manager**
Bryony Peach	**Stage Manager**
Kate Eccles	**Deputy Stage Manager**
Josie Thomas	**Costume Supervisor**
Kat Day-Smith	**Wardrobe Mistress**
Barry Abbotts	**Production Electrician**
Sam Smallman	**Lighting Programmer**
Samuel Clarkson	**Production Sound**
Cameron Naylor	**Production Video**
Jay Summers and JJ Smith	**Production Carpenters**
Jake Hughes	**Lighting Operator**
Karen Rao	**Deer Headdress Maker**

Joe Public	**Marketing and Sales Directors**
www.joepublicmarketing.com	
Borkowski PR	**Press**

Cast Biographies

Mark Extance | *The Bishop of Tatchester and Train Conductor*

Mark trained at the London Centre for Theatre Studies.

Theatre credits include: *Don Juan in Soho* (Wyndhams Theatre); *Correspondence* (Old Red Lion Theatre); *Three Days in the Country. London Assurance* (National Theatre); *A Midsummer Night's Dream* (Squerryes Court, Westerham); *Play of Thrones* (Union Theatre); *Marriage* (Belgrade Theatre); *Scenes from an Execution, Travelling Light* (National Theatre); *Yes Prime Minister* (UK tour and West End); (National Theatre); *School for Scandal* and *Dr Faustus* (Greenwich Theatre); *And Then There Were None* (UK tour); *Pygmalion* (Old Vic and Hong Kong Arts Festival); *Uncle Vanya* (English Touring Theatre); *Old Times* (Theatre Royal Bath); *Waiting for Godot, You Never Can Tell* (Peter Hall Company, UK tour and West End); *The Importance of Being Earnest* (Green Room Theatre Company); *Venice Preserv'd* (Arcola); *Much Ado About Nothing* (Jermyn St Theatre).

Josefina Gabrielle | *Pouncer and Caroline Louisa*

Josefina trained at the Arts Educational Schools London and began her career as a soloist with the National Ballet of Portugal.

Theatre credits include: *Stepping Out* (Vaudeville Theatre); *Charlie and the Chocolate Factory* (Theatre Royal Drury Lane); *Two into One* (Menier Chocolate Factory); Puss in Boots (Hackney Empire); *Merrily We Roll Along* (Menier Chocolate Factory, Harold Pinter Theatre and Digital Theatre – Olivier Award nomination for Best Supporting Actress); *The King and I* (UK tour – MTA nomination for Best Actress in a Visiting Company); *Park Avenue Cat* (Arts); *Me And My Girl* (Sheffield Crucible); *Sweet Charity* (Menier Chocolate Factory and Theatre Royal Haymarket – Clarence Derwent Award winner and Olivier Award nomination for Best Supporting Actress); *Hello, Dolly!* (Regent's Park Open Air Theatre); *The Murder Game* (King's Head); *The 39 Steps* (Criterion); *Red Peppers, The Astonished Heart, Family Album, Hands Across the Sea, Fumed Oak, Shadow Play* (Minerva Theatre, Chichester); *Singin' in the Rain* (Sadler's Wells and Leicester Haymarket Theatres); *A Chorus Line* (Sheffield Crucible); *The Witches of Eastwick* (Prince of Wales); *Chicago* (Adelphi and Cambridge Theatres); *Sunday in the Park with George* (Leicester Haymarket); *A Midsummer Night's Dream* (Cannizaro Park); *Oklahoma!* (National and Lyceum Theatres, Gershwin Theatre, New York – nominated for Olivier Award and Outer Critics Circle Award for Best Actress in a Musical and Astaire Award for Outstanding Dance); *A Chorus Line* (UK tour); *The Goodbye Girl* (Albery Theatre); *A Chorus Line* (Derby Playhouse); *Fame* (Cambridge Theatre); *Oklahoma!* (UK tour); *Carousel* (National Theatre/Shaftesbury Theatre).

Television and film credits include: *Miranda, Doctors, Ronnie Ancona and Co, Heartbeat, Totally Frank, Born and Bred, Auf Wiedersehen Pet, Sunburn* and *Oklahoma!*

Radio credits include: *In Tune; Blindness; Friday Night Is Music Night.*

Safiyya Ingar | *Maria*

Safiyya trained at Arts Educational Schools, London and she graduated in 2017.

Theatre credits include: *Growth* (Paines Plough, UK tour).

Theatre credits while training, include: *The Crucible*, *The Frontline*, *Sonny*.

Tom Kanji | *Charles and the Inspector of Police*

Theatre credits include: *Fiddler on the Roof*, *Romeo and Juliet*, *The Story Giant*, *The Sum* (Liverpool Everyman Rep); *Romeo and Juliet*, *Antony and Cleopatra*, *Much Ado About Nothing* (Hollywood Bowl/Barbican, Shakespeare's Globe, LA Philharmonic and BBC Symphony Orchestras); *The Winter's Tale*, *Pericles*, *Romeo and Juliet*, *Julius Caesar*, *Doctor Scroggy's War* (Shakespeare's Globe, Sam Wanamaker Playhouse and tours); *Eternal Love* (Shakespeare's Globe/ English Touring Theatre); *Cadfael – the Virgin in the Ice* (Middle Ground Theatre); *Much Ado About Nothing, Twelfth Night* (Ludlow Festival); *A Russian Play* (Lion and Unicorn); *Hamlet* (Northern Broadsides); *Othello*, *The Importance of Being Ernest* (RMS QM2 RADA); *Wild Horses* (Theatre 503); *Back of the Throat* (Old Red Lion); *The Girl the Oil Pipe and the Murder in the Forum*, *The Tempest* (Tara Arts and tours); *Prints of Denmark* (Edinburgh Fringe); *Les Liaisons Dangereuses* (New Vic Stoke); *Indian Ink* (Salisbury Playhouse).

Television includes: *Tyrant* (Fox TV); *Silent Witness* (BBC); *Hustle* (BBC); *Midnight Man* (Carnival Film); *Saddam's Tribe* (Channel 4).

Matthew Kelly | *Cole Hawlings and Abner Brown*

Matthew trained as an actor at the Manchester Polytechnic School of Theatre, going on to work in repertory and major regional theatres across the country. He has appeared several times in the West End, as the original Stanley in *Funny Peculiar*, a role he had created at the Liverpool Everyman, in *Waiting For Godot* with Ian McKellan and Roger Rees, Tim Firth's play *Sign of the Times*, the musical *Lend Me a Tenor!* and as Lennie in the Birmingham Repertory Theatre production of *Of Mice and Men* at the Savoy Theatre, where his performance won him the Olivier Award for Best Actor.

Most recent theatre credits include: *Desire Under the Elms* (Sheffield Crucible); *Pride and Prejudice* (Regent's Park Theatre and UK tour); *The Jew of Malta*, *Volpone*, *Love's Sacrifice* (RSC); *TOAST* (Park Theatre and 59E59, New York), *Twelfth Night* (Liverpool Everyman); *The History Boys* (Sheffield Crucible); *To Sir With Love* (Northampton and UK tour); *God of Carnage* (Nuffield Theatre, Southampton); *The Seagull* (Southwark Playhouse); *Educating Rita* (Menier Chocolate Factory, on tour and Edinburgh Festival); the musicals *Spamalot* and *Legally Blonde* (UK tours); *Troilus and Cressida* (Shakespeare's Globe); *Mirandolina* (Manchester Royal Exchange); *Amadeus* (Wilton's Music Hall); *Oh What a Lovely War!* (Octagon, Bolton); *Endgame* (Liverpool Everyman); *Who's Afraid of Virginia Woolf?* (Trafalgar Studios, London).

Television credits include: the award-winning thriller *Cold Blood*; *Benidorm*; *Bleak House*; *Egypt: The Pharaoh and the Showman*; *The Temple of the Sands*; *MI High*; *Moving On*; *Marple*; *Casualty*; *Heartbeat*; *My Family at War* and the documentary series *Forensic Casebook* – although he is probably best known for presenting *You Bet!* and *Stars in Their Eyes*.

Samuel Simmonds | *Peter*

Samuel graduated from ArtsEd in June 2017. Since finishing he has played Claudio in Oxford Shakespeare Company's *Much Ado About Nothing* and also appeared in BBC's *Doctors*.

ArtsEd credits include: *Let the Right One In*, *Sonny*, *Birdland* and *Starburst*.

Rosalind Steele | *Herne the Hunter, Rat and Abner's Head*

Rosalind trained at the Bristol Old Vic Theatre School.

Theatre credits include: *Fanny Hill and The Lost World* (Bristol Old Vic); *As You Like It* (Oxford Shakespeare Company); *William Wordsworth, Swallows and Amazons, Rogue Herries* (Theatre by the Lake, Keswick); *Father Christmas* (Lyric Hammersmith); *Dick Whittington* (Key Theatre); *We Didn't Mean to Go to Sea, Margaret Catchpole, Parkway Dreams, Sid and Hetty* (Eastern Angles); *The Snail and the Whale* (Tall Stories and US tour/Broadway); *The Merchant of Venice, A Midsummer Night's Dream* (GB Theatre and UK tour); *Daisy Pulls it Off* and *Arabian Nights* (Watermill Theatre, Newbury); *Sam Rose in the Shadows, The Golden Cowpat, Tim and Light* (Tucked In and UK tour) and regular appearances at Shakespeare's Globe as part of the *Read Not Dead* series.

Rosalind is also a Musical Director and Composer, and has composed for *Read Not Dead* at Shakespeare's Globe, GB Theatre, Tucked In Productions and RBL Theatre Company, for whom she is the associate composer.

Alistair Toovey | *Kay*

Theatre credits include: *An Octoroon* (Orange Tree Theatre); *Richard III* (Finnish National Theatre); *French Without Tears* (Orange Tree Theatre); *Crossing Jerusalem* (Park Theatre/Pascal Theatre Company); *Mind the Gap* (National Theatre); *Lord of the Flies* (Regent's Park Open Air Theatre); *Cake* (Edinburgh Festival Fringe); *Les Miserables* (Cameron Mackintosh Ltd).

Television credits include: *Silent Witness* (BBC); *Tut* (Muse Entertainment Enterprises/Spike TV).

Film credits include: *The Choke* (MWP Media).

Company Biographies

Piers Torday | *Writer*

A former theatre and television producer, Piers's bestselling first book for children, *The Last Wild* was shortlisted for the Waterstones Children's Book Award and has been translated into over 13 languages. His second book, *The Dark Wild*, won the Guardian Children's Fiction Prize. The son of the late Paul Torday (*Salmon Fishing in the Yemen*) Piers recently completed his father's final unfinished novel, *The Death of an Owl*. Other books include *The Wild Beyond* and *There May Be A Castle*. He has written short stories for *A Wisp of Wisdom*, *Winter Magic* and *Scoop*. A judge for this year's Costa Children's Book Award, he is also a Trustee of the Pleasance Theatre and the Ministry of Stories.

Justin Audibert | *Director*

Justin is a freelance theatre director.

Recent directing credits include: *Macbeth/Winter's Tale* (NT Learning); *Beowolf* (Unicorn Theatre); *The Cardinal* (Southwark Playhouse); *Snow in Midsummer* (RSC); *Macbeth* (NT Learning); *My Mother Medea* (Unicorn Theatre); *How Not to Live in Suburbia* (Pulse Festival, Summerhall); *The Man with the Hammer* (Plymouth Theatre Royal); *Flare Path* (Birdsong Productions and Original Theatre Company); *Mind the Gap* (New Views winner, National Theatre Temporary Theatre); *The Jew of Malta* (RSC); *Beached* (Marlowe Theatre, Soho Theatre); *Hamlet* (Watermill Theatre); *Wingman* (Soho Theatre, Pleasance); *Raymondo* (Battersea Arts Centre, Summerhall and Pulse Festival); *World Enough and Time* (Papatango New Writing Prizewinner); *Unscorched* (Finborough Theatre); *The Fu Manchu Complex* (Oval House); *A Season in the Congo: Parallel Project* (Clare, Young Vic); *Wrong Un* (Red Ladder); *Gruesome Playground Injuries* (Gate Theatre); *The Tempest* (RSC Shakespeare in a Suitcase); *Future Regrets* (live theatre/RSC); *Armley the Musical* (Interplay); *Company Along the Mile* (West Yorkshire Playhouse, Arcola).

Justin co-wrote and co-presented the *BBC Live Lessons* on Shakespeare for the Royal Shakespeare Company. He is an Artistic Associate for NT Connections, a Creative Associate for the Shakespeare Schools Festival, an Education Associate Practitioner for the Royal Shakespeare Company and an Associate of Wilton's Music Hall. In 2012 he was the recipient of the Leverhulme Award for Emerging Directors from the National Theatre Studio.

Tom Piper | *Designer*

Recent theatre designs include: *Boudica* (Shakespeare's Globe); *Bayadere* (Shobana Jeyasingh Dance, Sadler's Wells); *Pelléas et Melisande, Eugene Onegin* (Garsington Opera); *Rhinoceros, Hay Fever* (Royal Lyceum); *Frankenstein, Hedda Gabler* (Northern Stage); *iHo* (Hampstead Theatre); *Harrogate* (HighTide, Royal Court); *Pride and Prejudice* (Regent's Park Open Air Theatre and UK tour); *A Midsummer Night's Dream* (RSC and UK tour); *Carmen La Cubana* (Chatelet, Paris); *Endgame, Lear, Hamlet, Libertine* (Citizens Theatre); *Red Velvet* (West End, Tricycle Theatre, New York); *A Wolf in Snakeskin Shoes, The House That Will Not Stand* (Tricycle Theatre); *The King's Speech* (Birmingham Rep, Chichester Festival Theatre, UK tour); *Orfeo* (ROH); *Tamburlaine* (Theatre for a New Audience, New York); *Zorro* (West End, UK tour, Paris, Moscow, Amsterdam, Tokyo, Atlanta); *Goodbye to All That, Vera, Vera, Vera* (Royal Court, Theatre Local).

As Associate Designer of the RSC, Tom designed over thirty of their shows including *The Histories* for which he won an Olivier for Best Costume Design.

Tom designed *Blood Swept Lands and Seas of Red* at the Tower of London and received an MBE for services to Theatre and First World War Commemorations. Other recent exhibitions include: *Dr Blighty* (Nutkhut); *Curtain Up* (V&A, Lincoln Centre New York): *Blood* (Jewish Museum); *Staging the World* (Shakespeare Exhibition as part of the Cultural Olympiad, British Museum).

Anna Watson | *Lighting Designer*

Theatre lighting design includes: *The Seagull, Shopping and Fucking* (Lyric Hammersmith); *King Lear* (Shakespeare's Globe); *Snow in Midsummer, Roaring Girl* (RSC); *Dutchman, The Secret Agent, Fireface, Disco Pigs, Sus* (Young Vic); *You for Me for You, Plaques and Tangles, A Time to Reap* (Royal Court); *The Chronicles of Kalki, Sisters* (Gate Theatre); *Bank on it* (Theatre-Rites/Barbican); *Salt, Root and Roe* (Donmar at Trafalgar Studios); *On the Record, It Felt Empty When the Heart Went at First, But it's Alright Now* (Arcola); *Paradise, Salt* (Ruhr Triennale, Germany); *Gambling, This Wide Night* (Soho Theatre); *Rutherford and Son, Ruby Moon* (Northern Stage); *King Pelican* and *Speed Death of the Radiant Child* (Drum, Plymouth).

Opera lighting design includes: *Don Carlo* (Grange Park); *Orlando* (Welsh National Opera/Scottish Opera); *Ruddigore* (Barbican, Opera North and UK tour); *Critical Mass* (Almeida); *Songs from a Hotel Bedroom, Tongue Tied* (Linbury, Royal Opera House); *The Bartered Bride* (Royal College of Music); *Against Oblivion* (Toynbee Hall).

Dance lighting design includes: *Mothers* and *Soul Play* (The Place); *Refugees of a Septic Heart* (The Garage); *View from the Shore* and *Animule Dance* (Clore, Royal Opera House).

Ed Lewis | *Composer and Sound Designer*

Edward studied Music at Oxford University and subsequently trained as a composer and sound designer at the Bournemouth Media School. He works in theatre, film, television and radio. He has recently been nominated for several Off West End Theatre Awards, and films he has recently worked on have won several awards at the LA International Film Festival and Filmstock International Film Festival.

Recent theatre sound design includes: *The Resistible Rise of Arturo Ui* (Donmar Warehouse); *The Best Man* (Bill Kenwright Productions); *Scarlett* (Hampstead Theatre/Theatr Clwyd); *Fool For Love, Unfaithful, Bug, The Dazzle* (Found 111); *The Vertical Hour, Remarkable Invisible* (Theatre by the Lake, Keswick); *Baddies The Musical, Breaking The Ice, Hannah, Medea* (Unicorn Theatre); *Chef* (Soho Theatre); *Abigail's Party* (The Curve, Leicester); *The Cement Garden* (VAULT Festival); *The Speed Twins, Slowly, Hurts Given and Received, Apple Pie* (Riverside Studios); *Eugenie Grandet* (Hartshorn-Hook Productions); *Cuddles* (Oval House); *Molly Sweeney* (Print Room/Lyric Hammersmith); *Ignorance* (Hampstead Theatre); *Gravity* (Birmingham Rep); *A Midsummer Night's Dream* (Almeida); *Thom Pain* (Print Room); *On The Rocks, Amongst Friends, Darker Shores* (Hampstead Theatre); *Measure For Measure* (Sherman Theatre, Cardiff); *Emo* (Bristol Old Vic/Young Vic); *Once Upon a Time in Wigan, 65 Miles* (Paines Plough/Hull Truck Theatre); *Krapp's Last Tape, Spoonface Steinberg* (Hull Truck Theatre); *The Shallow End* (Southwark Playhouse); *I Am Falling* (Sadler's Wells/Gate Theatre); *Orpheus and Eurydice, Quartet* (Old Vic Tunnels); *The Beloved* (Bush Theatre); *The Stronger, The Pariah, Boy with a Suitcase, Walking the Tightrope, Le Marriage, Meetings* (Arcola); *Hedda, Breathing Irregular* (Gate Theatre); *Le Grand Mort, Madness In Valencia* (Trafalgar Studios); *The Madness of George III, Kalagora, Macbeth* (UK tours).

Nina Dunn | *Video Designer*

Theatre includes: *Cookies* (Theatre Royal Haymarket); *Forty Years On* (Chichester Festival Theatre); *Alice's Adventures Underground* (Les Enfants Terribles/Emma Brunjes Productions); *The Seven Acts of Mercy* and *Volpone* (RSC); *Rocky Horror Show* (European tour); *A Little Night Music* (RADA); *The Mountaintop* (Young Vic); *No Man's Land* (UK tour/West End); *The Damned United* (West Yorkshire Playhouse/UK tour); Diary of a Teenage Girl (Southwark Playhouse); *The Hook* (Royal and Derngate); *The Merchant of Venice (Almeida)*; *Usagi Yojimbo* (Southwark Playhouse*)*; *Minetti* (Edinburgh International Festival); *Phantom of The Opera* (UK and US tours).

Opera includes: Verdi's *Macbeth* (Vienna State Opera); *La Traviata* (Glyndebourne); *Hippolyte et Aricie* (Glyndebourne); *La Bohème* (Welsh National Opera); *The Flying Dutchman (*English National Opera*)*; *Faust, A Midsummer Night's Dream* and *Die Frau Ohne Schatten* (Mariinsky Theatre).

Nina also lectures at RADA and other higher education institutions.

Simon Pittman | *Movement Director*

Simon is a movement director, theatre director, and an associate director at Frantic Assembly.

Theatre movement direction includes: *Out of the Cage* (Park Theatre/Rose Theatre Kingston); *The Go-Between* (Apollo Theatre); *The Kingdom* (Soho Theatre); *The White Bike* (The Space); *The Shawshank Redemption* (Edinburgh Festival and Gaiety Theatre, Dublin); *Romeo and Juliet, The Caucasian Chalk Circle* (National Youth Theatre Wales/Frantic Assembly); *Between Two Worlds* (Sherman Theatre, Cardiff); *Mixter Maxter, 99 . . . 100* (National Theatre of Scotland).

As Associate: *365* (Edinburgh International Festival/National Theatre of Scotland); *The Curious Incident of The Dog in the Night-time* (Gielgud Theatre).

Theatre direction includes: *Othello* (National Youth Theatre of Great Britain/Frantic Assembly, Ambassadors, West End); *The Soldier's Tale* (Rough Fiction/London Arts Orchestra – tour); *Not a Game for Boys* (Library Theatre Manchester); *His Wild Imaginings* (Rough Fiction at LSO St Luke's); *The Last of the Lake* (Brighton Dome, UK tour); *The Love of the Nightingale* (UK tour).

As Associate: *The Go-Between* (West Yorkshire Playhouse); *Floyd Collins* (Southwark Playhouse); *The Shawshank Redemption* (Edinburgh Festival/Gaiety Theatre, Dublin).

Simon trained on the Birkbeck Theatre Directing MFA and as movement associate to Steven Hoggett and Scott Graham. He was resident director at the Library Theatre, Manchester 2006/07, co-directs the ensemble company Rough Fiction and is a selector for the National Student Drama Festival.

Samuel Wyer | *Puppetry Designer*

Samuel Wyer is a puppet-maker, theatre designer and illustrator. His creative practice when designing and making puppets focuses heavily on texture and character, bringing them to life with the illustrated approach synonymous with his set design work.

Puppet designer/maker credits include: *How to Hide a Lion* (Polka Theatre); *The Bear* (Pins and Needles Productions); *The House Where Winter Lives* (Punchdrunk); *A Christmas Carol* and *The Jabberwocky* (Petersham Playhouse); *Peepshow* (Twice Shy Theatre).

Set and puppet designer credits include: *The Terrible Infants, The Trench, Dinner at the Twits, The Marvellous Imaginary Menagerie, The Vaudevillians* (Les Enfants Terribles); *Goosebumps Alive!* (The Vaults); *Ragnarök* (Eastern Angles).

Set and costume designer credits include: *The Elephantom* (National Theatre, Gyre and Gimble); *The Hartlepool Monkey* (Gyre and Gimble); *Alice's Adventures Underground, The Game's Afoot, The Sherlock Holmes Experience* (Les Enfants Terribles); *Under the Eiderdown* and *The Space Invaders Agency* (Punchdrunk).

Vicky Richardson | *Casting Director*

Vicky is currently Associate Casting Director at the Manchester Royal Exchange and was previously Casting Associate at the Donmar Warehouse.

Theatre casting director credits include: *Of Kith and Kin* (Sheffield Crucible/Bush Theatre); *Desire Under the Elms* (Sheffield Crucible); *Macbeth, Romeo and Juliet, I Want My Hat Back* (National Theatre); *Breaking the Code* (Royal Exchange, Manchester); *Run the Beast Down* (Finborough Theatre); *Henry IV* (Donmar Warehouse/St Ann's Warehouse, New York); *Constellations* (Singapore Rep Theatre); *House* and *Amongst the Reeds* (Clean Break); *Archipelago* (Lighthouse, Poole); *Dinner with Friends* (Park Theatre); *Debris* (Southwark Playhouse).

As co-casting director: *Our Town, Persuasion, Twelfth Night* (Royal Exchange, Manchester); *Parliament Square* (Royal Exchange, Manchester/Bush Theatre); *The Resistible Rise of Arturo Ui, Versailles* (Donmar Warehouse); *Shakespeare Trilogy* (Donmar Warehouse/St Ann's Warehouse); *Dedication* (Nuffield, Southampton).

As casting consultant: *Misalliance, Low Level Panic, Each His Own Wilderness* and *Buckets* (Orange Tree Theatre); *Blue Heart* (Bristol Tobacco Factory/Orange Tree Theatre).

About Wilton's Music Hall

A rough East End diamond . . . exquisite: a building that speaks back and forth between the nineteenth and twenty-first centuries, and between beauty and racketiness, with real grace . . . The building is a five-star delight.

Lyn Gardner, *The Guardian*, 2015

Wilton's is of international significance as it is the only surviving Grand Music Hall in the world. Wilton's has been a Grade II* listed building since 1971 and is situated in a conservation area.

The music hall was built in 1858 by the entrepreneur John Wilton. John also procured the Prince of Denmark pub, otherwise (and still) known as the Mahogany Bar and adjoining houses. The building opened in 1859 to much acclaim with some of the great music-hall stars such as Champagne Charlie and Arthur Lloyd regularly performing. Due to Wilton's location near the docks there was an international cast and audience alike.

In the 1880s fire regulations changed and Eilton's closed as a music hall and was purchased by a Wesleyan Mission and used by them until the 1950s, during which time they:

- Fed 2,000 people a day during the Dockers strike of 1889;
- Housed the first Ethiopian working men's club in 1920s;
- Supported the East End anti-fascists in the 1930s providing a safe haven during the Battle of Cable Street in 1936;
- Ran free Sunday activities for local children and gave them free fruit;
- Ran free cinema screenings for the local community;
- Offered skills training in sewing, woodwork and literacy;
- Offered shelter in World War I and World War II for the people of East London.

The Methodists departed in 1950 and the building fell into disrepair despite a failed restoration attempt in the 1980s, which actually left the building gutted and structurally dangerous.

In 2017 the picture has changed somewhat. In 2015 we completed a three-year Heritage Lottery Funded capital project, which has conserved the hall, maintaining the beautiful barley-twist columns and the handsome balcony. After the completion of work on the Hall the houses were then restored ensuring that Wilton's had more front-of-house and commercial

space as well as dedicated learning facilities. The rooms now are made up of: the Mahogany Bar, the John Wilton Room (a heritage and exhibition space), the Cocktail Bar, the Champagne Charlie Room, the Study and the Aldgate and Allhallows Learning and Participation Studio.

Wilton's is now home to a year-round programme of exceptional live music and vibrant theatre productions targeted at our local community, wider London, national and international audiences. Our building is now open and accessible every weekday, with an affordable artistic programme running all year round which in the last year has included work by: BBC Proms, Royal Opera House, English Touring Theatre, Shakespeare at Tobacco Factory, Watermill Theatre and Les Enfants Terribles to name but a few.

Wilton's has also offered a lot to a number of films as a unique, historic setting. Not only does this mean that Wilton's has been immortalised in a range of extraordinary films ensuring the building's historic splendour is shared with a much wider public but the hires from such films have enabled Wilton's to continually subsidise our artistic and community programmes. Some of the films shot at Wilton's include: *Bleak House; Chaplin; Dancing on the Edge; De-Lovely; Dorian Gray; Interview with the Vampire: The Vampire Chronicles; Kiss Kiss (Bang Bang); Mr Selfridge; Muppets Most Wanted; Nicholas Nickleby; Penelope; Sherlock Holmes: A Game of Shadows; Suffragette; The Grave Matter of Notorious Serial Killers Burke and Hare; The Krays; The Importance of Being Earnest* and others.

Wilton's has always been an exceptional place for an audience to hear live music but we have also built up a reputation for world-class musicians recording their music videos in the space such as: Marc Almond, Adam Ant, Billy Bragg, Kate Bush The Coral, Bryan Ferry, Frankie Goes to Hollywood Kelis, Kwabs, Laura Marling, Mumford and Sons, Paul Nutini, Frank Turner, and Wild Beasts.

For more information about Wilton's Music Hall visit
www.wiltons.org.uk

Wilton's Music Hall

Hero Productions

Executive Producer Simon Wheeler
Company Directors Judy Naake and Hermione Norris

Hero Film and TV is predominantly a film and TV production company set up by
Simon Wheeler (*Castles in the Sky*, *Buddha in Suburbia*, *Kingdom*, *Wire in the
Blood*, *Darwin: Evolution*), to create content for the UK and US market.

The Box of Delights is a long held passion of Simon's, and Hero is delighted
to present this first-ever stage adaptation in such a unique and beautiful venue.

Supporters

Wilton's is a charity, running a world-class artistic programme that is accessible to
everyone through affordable tickets prices and free activities for our local community.

We wouldn't be alive and thriving today if it wasn't for our wonderful group of
supporters and friends. Thank you for all of your support, ensuring our magical
legacy lives on for generations to come.

The Box of Delights Supporters

Adnams
Nidaa Ghazal and Maxime Hennequet
Peter Kerwood
Lansons
Royal Victoria Hall Foundation

The Box of Delights Production Thanks

Set up Scenery   Stage and Sound Services
Chris Fisher   Illusion Adviser
Transform Draping
Cosprop, Chichester Festival Theatre and Drama Studio
for costume hires
Darren Ware   Wigs

Wilton's Supporters

Aldgate and Allhallows Foundation
Alex and Susan de Mont
Alison Kirby
Andrew Lloyd Webber Foundation
Astell Scientific
Barbara Whent
Bernard Sunley Foundation
Berwin Leighton Paisner
Canary Wharf Group PLC
Caroline and Roger Dix
Carolyn Saunders
Chris Bartram
City Bridge Trust
Clyde Cooper
David Crook
Dr and Mrs Gayner
Financial Times
Foundation for Sports and the Arts
Foyle Foundation
Garfield Weston Foundation
George and Ann Marsh
Heritage Lottery Fund
Ian Salter
Ince & Co
Inga Beale
Jeremy Hargrove
Kate Bonner
Kestrelman Trust
Kiffer and Allison Weisselberg
Lansons

Lord and Lady Francis
  and Nathalie Phillimore
Louise Hodges
McKinsey & Company
Michael O'Callaghan
Mike Kavanagh and Mark Aspery
Nick and Chris Hunn
Nidaa Ghazal
  and Maxime Hennequet
Revd David Rogers
Rogers Stirk Harbour +Partners
  Charitable Foundation
Royal Victoria Hall Foundation
Sarah Mansell
SITA Trust
Stephen and Linda Simpson
The Boris Karloff Charitable Trust
The D'Oyly Carte Charitable Trust
The Loveday Charitable Trust
The Mackintosh Foundation
The Noël Coward Foundation
The Peter Wolff Trust
The Sackler Trust
The Williams Charitable Trust
Trinity Bouy Wharf Trust
Unity Theatre Trust
Viridor Credits Landfill Communities
  Fund
White Light Ltd
Wolfson Foundation

And all our donors who wish to remain anonymous

Wilton's Honorary Patrons

Marc Almond
Henry Goodman
Rosamund Pike

www.wiltons.org.uk/support

The Box of Delights

Piers Torday began his career in theatre and then
television as a producer and writer. His first book for
children, *The Last Wild*, was shortlisted for the
Waterstones Children's Book Award. The sequel, *The
Dark Wild*, won the Guardian Children's Fiction Prize.
Other books include *The Wild Beyond*, *The Death of
an Owl* (with Paul Torday) and *There May Be a Castle*,
which was nominated for the Carnegie Medal. He lives
in London with his husband and a very naughty dog.

John Masefield (1878–1967) was the fifteenth Poet
Laureate, and author of over sixty-two collections of
poetry, twenty-three plays, seventeen novels and seven
books for children, among other work. His poems
include *Sea-Fever*, *Cargoes*, *The Everlasting Mercy*,
Salt-Water Ballads and *Reynard the Fox*. Among
his plays are *The Campden Wonder*, *The Tragedy of
Pompey the Great* and *Good Friday*. Books for children
include *A Book of Discoveries*, *The Midnight Folk* and
The Box of Delights or When the Wolves Were Running,
which has been adapted several times for radio and
television, and received its world premiere on stage at
Wilton's Music Hall in 2017. Masefield was awarded the
Order of Merit in 1937, and was the first president of
the Society of Authors. His ashes are buried in Poet's
Corner at Westminster Abbey.

PIERS TORDAY

The Box of Delights

based on the novel by
JOHN MASEFIELD

FABER & FABER

First published in 2017
by Faber and Faber Ltd
74–77 Great Russell Street
London WC1B 3DA

Typeset by Country Setting, Kingsdown, Kent CT14 8ES
Printed in England by CPI Group (UK) Ltd, Croydon CR0 4YY

A CIP record for this book
is available from the British Library

978-0-571-34610-3

Adaptor's Note

The second of Poet Laureate John Masefield's only two books for children, *The Box of Delights* (1935) is a loose companion piece to *The Midnight Folk* (1927). Both novels pit orphan schoolboy Kay Harker against the greed, cunning and dark powers of the sorcerer Abner Brown and his bewitching associate Sylvia Daisy Pouncer.

Born in 1878, Masefield met Algernon Swinburne as a young man, and lived to see Philip Larkin published. With a foot in both the Victorian and the modern age, part of the *Box*'s timeless appeal is its genre-busting combination of classic children's adventure – ancient folkloric magic, Christmas feasts and talking animals – with bang up-to-date thrills: criminal gangs, cars that turn into aeroplanes and, of course, teleportation.

Masefield, described by Muriel Spark in her biography as a 'born storyteller', honed those narrative skills in his early life as a sailor. On board HMS *Conway* he read *Treasure Island* and walked on deck with characters drawn straight from its pages. In fact the book has the elastic, eccentric and winning charm of a nautical yarn being spun, yet like so many such spontaneous entertainments, it has matured into a much-loved legend, due in no small part to a fondly remembered 1980s BBC TV adaptation.

The story springs from a very simple idea Masefield had: would it ever be possible to stop a cathedral service happening? He drew directly on his childhood for inspiration. Like the children's guardian in the story, his own mother was called Caroline. Like Kay Harker, he too was orphaned at an early age, and the central location of Seekings House was based on the rambling family manorial home he moved into after his grandfather died. In doing so, he created the first entirely original children's adventure of the twentieth century, blending the folkloric mysticism of Albion with the more lurid criminalities of the Jazz Age.

As an early landmark in children's publishing, we still see the book's influence everywhere today. While the plucky band of young children and magical phoenix are straight out of E. Nesbit, there are definite shades of Cole Hawlings in Albus Dumbledore, and Pouncer is a direct forerunner of Roald Dahl's Grand High Witch. Masefield was talking about deep magic long before C. S. Lewis, and his enthralling introduction to children of the concepts of time and space paved the way for some of Phillip Pullman's more metaphysical ambitions.

We have taken this much-loved, fearlessly original classic, and tried to give it a new theatrical life appropriate for today's young audience. While all the stage time in the world could not do justice to Masefield's inventiveness, in just two hours we hope to showcase the wickedest lines of his impish humour, the most visionary set pieces of his fantasy, and the most thrilling cliffhanger moments of his adventure. Which in the end, is all about a young boy who has just a few days to save Christmas, because – on stage as in life – the dark wolves of history are running. Will he escape their bite?

Piers Torday
November 2017

The Box of Delights, a Wilton's Music Hall and Hero Productions Commission, was first performed at Wilton's Music Hall, London, on 1 December 2017. The cast, in alphabetical order, was as follows:

Bishop of Tatchester / Train Conductor Mark Extance
Sylvia Daisy Pouncer / Caroline Louisa Josefina Gabrielle
Maria Jones Safiyya Ingar
Charles / Inspector of Police Tom Kanji
Cole Hawlings / Abner Brown Matthew Kelly
Peter Jones Samuel Simmonds
Herne the Hunter / Rat / Abner's Head Rosalind Steele
Kay Harker Alastair Toovey

Director Justin Audibert
Designer Tom Piper
Lighting Designer Anna Watson
Composer and Sound Designer Ed Lewis
Video Designer Nina Dunn
Movement Director Simon Pittman
Puppetry Designer Samuel Wyer
Casting Director Vicky Richardson

Characters

Rogers
the Bishop's Butler

Train Conductor

THE WOLVES

Charles
a con man and jewel thief

Sylvia Daisy Pouncer
a witch

THE ANIMALS

Toby
a Toby dog

A Rat

A Phoenix and her Baby

Woodland Creatures

Carol Singers, Wolves, Reporters

ACT ONE

The strange events leading up to Christmas
in the small market town of Condicote, 1938

ACT TWO

Christmas!

THE BOX OF DELIGHTS

THE BOX OF DELIGHTS

Act One

ONE
KAY'S DREAM

Christmas, six years ago. The Harker family home. A home for paintings – a family portrait, a rural landscape, and a piano.
Carol Singers gather in the snow outside.

Carol Singers (*singing*)
And this I ask, and fain would know
Will Now be in a day or so?
Is this-time-next-year Now or no?
Or did Now happen a long time ago?

Long, long ago
Or did Now happen a long time ago?
Long, long ago

And was Tomorrow yesterday?
Or had it been and gone Today?
Will no one say?
I wish someone would say . . .

The fire crackles up into a roar.
Kay just manages to rescue the landscape.
His parents are frozen in time, in their portrait.

Long, long ago
Or did Now happen a long time ago?
Long, Long ago . . .

The singers melt into the shadows.
Kay is all alone.

Kay I have always believed in dreams. Sometimes I dream Mother and Father are here again. We are a family again once more. I used to have this dream a lot. At the end of every year, because that was when . . .

Kay's parents have now disappeared.

But that was long ago. That *life* was long ago.
Now I go away to school, and stay with my guardian Caroline Louisa at Seekings in the holidays.
I still dream though.
So many dreams.

We hear a steam train start in background, very powerful and loud.

And no dream I ever saw –

The train grows louder and faster.

Was quite as strange as the one I had –
This Christmas!

A shriek of whistle, white steam pours across the stage, as a train appears.
Along with some train passengers, who together make a carriage and settle into a comfortable rhythm. As the smoke clears and the wintry countryside begins to rattle by outside, and we find . . .

TWO
CONDICOTE TRAIN

Kay, now on the train, curled up fast asleep.
Spiky silhouettes of castles and woods flicker past.

Conductor Tickets please! Tickets from Musborough Junction! (*Waking Kay.*) Tickets please, lad!

Toby, a Toby dog, appears.

Kay (*feeling his pockets*) I can't find it.

Conductor *Ticket* please, sir.

Kay I had it when we left Musborough . . .

Toby paws at Kay, sniffing.

Hello, boy . . . where did you come from? I don't suppose you know where my ticket is?

Toby bows down barking. Kay peers down and picks up his ticket.

You found it! Clever dog!

Conductor punches the ticket and moves on, not impressed.
And there, like magic, is Cole Hawlings, with a showman's trunk.

Cole I see that my Toby has made a new friend. For this is the time that likings are made.

Kay He found my ticket! That was close.

Cole No doubt it slipped out while you rumpaged.

Kay I must have fallen asleep. He saved Christmas for me all right. I don't know how to thank you.

Cole Perhaps one day I shall ask you to do the same.

Kay I don't understand. Do what?

Cole Save Christmas, Master Harker. Save Christmas, when the wolves are running!

Darkness as the train enters a tunnel. A wolf howls . . .
When they emerge, Cole and Toby have vanished. In their place are Charles, a wolf-faced clerical gentleman, and his companion, Sylvia Daisy Pouncer, wearing a veil and a wolf-fur stole.

Charles Going home for Christmas, ha-ha what?

Kay Where did that old man with a dog go?

Pouncer What old man? Dear child, it won't do to talk to strangers on trains. Not at such a . . . festive time of year. May I sit here, *Kay Harker*?

Kay Yes, but please – how do you know my name?

Pouncer It is my job to know things, and your job to listen. I am accompanying dear Charles here, who is visiting the Missionary College at Hope-le-Chesters for Christmas. Do you know it?

Kay I have heard of it.

Charles (*crossing himself*) Such a grave and holy place. Alas, I will never be as pious and good as the great Father Boddledale, its most reverend master, ha-ha what!

Pouncer You can but try, my dear. A little spoonful of piety at breakfast, that's what I always say . . . And a pinch of goodness at bedtime!

She laughs. It is not a nice experience for anyone.

Kay Please, what is your name . . . Have we met before?

Pouncer I don't believe we have had the pleasure, Mr Harker . . . and I would never forget such a . . . charming . . . little child.

Charles Now! What do you say to a little card trick? It is Christmas, after all, ha-ha what?

Kay I don't know . . .

Charles Well, you soon will! Now, my young friend, 'Follow the Lady'.

He shuffles a pack of cards.

Watch now the whirling cards . . . They shift, they lift, they dive . . . and now?

He deals three face down.

Which one is she?

Kay (*pointing*) That one.

Charles Didn't I tell you, my dear Pouncer, that he had a clever face?

Pouncer (*tracing Kay's face with a gloved finger*) *Such* a clever face! Not too clever a face, I trust? I don't approve of children being too clever.

Kay Please don't worry. My teachers tell me I am too dreamy to be clever.

Charles (*moving on*) Now, my young knight, shall we add some incentive? If you beat me again, you shall have a sixpence. But if I beat you, you shall give me half a crown. A deal, ha-ha what?

Kay gets out his wallet.

Kay This is my Christmas pocket money.

Pouncer And such a lot of money for one so young, all on their own. Promise me you will take great care of it, Mr Harker. There are always so many wicked people about at this time of year, preying on the unwary. One cannot be too careful!

Kay I am always very careful.

Pouncer Promise me you will be. I could not bear it if you were to be cruelly parted from so precious a sum. *Swear.*

Kay I swear!

Charles shuffles and deals again.

Charles Now, which one is the lady?

Kay looks down but the cards have all disappeared.

Kay They've gone! How did you do that?

Charles Magic, no doubt. Now, half a crown please. It will aid the Retired Rats Home at Condicote.

Pouncer (*holding out her hand*) A more deserving cause we do not know.

Kay gets out his wallet.

Kay (*hesitating*) Retired Rats?

Pouncer They grow very infirm in their old age.

Kay is not convinced. Pouncer snatches the coin, distracting him, while Charles lifts the boy's wallet from his pocket.

(*Taking Kay's hands.*) It's a terrible sight. Let us hope you are never subjected to it.

The train huffs to a halt.

Charles (*looking out of the window*) Ah – this is Condicote, is it not?

Pouncer Indeed it is. Our stop as well as Mr Harker's. (*Suddenly scheming.*) Where the hawks get out to wait for the chicken . . .

Kay Please, I still don't understand how you know all about me?

But they've gone. Then Kay pats himself.

My wallet!

The train melts away into the bustle of Condicote Station.

THREE
CONDICOTE STATION

A village station, quaint and peeling.
  Kay drags his trunk through the other passengers,
looking for his guardian Caroline Louisa, but instead . . .
  He finds the old man and his dog again, who have
appeared as if by magic.

Cole (*bowing to Kay*) Young master.

Kay Hello again. I thought you'd disappeared. (*Patting dog.*) Hello, boy! . . .

Cole Now that there is Toby, my Toby dog. And I am Cole Hawlings, at your service.

Cole doffs his hat. Kay awkwardly shakes his hand.

Kay I'm waiting for my guardian, Caroline Louisa. What brings you to Condicote?

Cole I suppose you could call me a wandering showman, of sorts.

Kay (*pointing to the case*) Like a Punch and Judy man?

Cole If you like . . . let me show you something that will make it clearer.

He gets out a small box from the case which catches the light.

Kay That looks very old.

Cole Older than you know.

Kay What's inside?

Cole Secrets. Magic secrets – that must not be had by those who crave their power. I think you know who I mean.

Cole locks the box away again.

Kay That vicar and his companion! They were looking for you . . . They must have stolen my wallet too. I'm such a duffer!

Cole Now, now Master Harker, of Seekings. None of that. But perhaps as you have seen that the wolves are running, you will do something to stop their bite?

Kay Wolves? I don't know . . . Caroline Louisa is waiting . . .

Cole No other soul can do this for me but you alone, Kay Harker.

Kay Why me?

Cole Because Christmas itself depends upon it.

Toby implores Kay adorably. Caroline Louisa arrives, kindly and flustered, looking for Kay in the crowd.

Caroline Kay? Kay?

Kay (*to Cole*) I'm sorry. I'm just a schoolboy. I think you must have mistaken me for someone else. That's my guardian. I should go.

Cole So be it. But when wolves run, it is better to know than not, Master Harker. If they come, you shall find me at The Drop of Dew. But now you must go. Time and tide and buttered eggs wait for no man!

Caroline There you are! I thought I'd never find you.

Kay Caroline Louisa!

They hug tight, a genuine bond.

And this is –

But Cole and Toby have vanished.

Oh! How strange.

Caroline What is? Oh, never mind. My darling Kay! Here at last and all is well with the world. I'm sorry to be late but there was a queue in the butcher's like you wouldn't believe. I was worried I might have missed you!

Kay I would never miss Christmas!

Caroline I know, and what a Christmas it is going to be . . . I promise.

Kay It nearly wasn't though . . . I lost my ticket, until a Toby dog found it, and then just now, a vicar stole all my pocket money.

Caroline A vicar? Are you quite sure?

Kay I swear on my life. He showed me a card trick, then made all the cards disappear.

Caroline Well I never. First the post office changed its opening hours, and now this. Condicote is just one surprise after another these days, I can't keep up, truly.

Kay He was a very strange vicar, and his friend was even stranger. They knew my name and address at Seekings.

Caroline Seekings is quite the local landmark, you know. And they could have spied that on your luggage labels. It's a very polite thing to do. Did you notice any other suspicious people on the train?

Kay Only this old man with a green baize case and an Irish terrier . . . The one who was here a moment ago.

Caroline Now come along, we mustn't be late – it's buttered eggs for tea.

Kay Buttered eggs! Mr Hawlings . . . He knew that too!

Caroline Who knew what?

Kay Nothing . . . it doesn't matter.

Caroline Well, let's worry no more about it in that case. Now, there's something else I should tell you. It might be rather a shock, I'm afraid. We have the Jones children staying with us as well.

Kay Maria?

Caroline Yes, with her brother Peter – their father has been posted to India.

Kay I do hope Maria has brought some pistols. She normally has one or two.

Caroline I hope she has brought nothing of the kind. Now COME ALONG!

Kay drags his case off after Caroline. The Conductor rings his station bell, as he and the passengers despatch them with 'Carol of the Bells', the station melting away into the cosy parlour of Seekings house . . .

Company
Hark how the bells,
sweet silver bells,
all seem to say,
throw cares away.

Christmas is here,
bringing good cheer,
to young and old,
meek and the bold.

Gaily they ring
while people sing
songs of good cheer,
Christmas is here!

*Caroline Louisa's and now Kay's home, a comfortable
and shabbily welcoming Tudor manor house that has
been haphazardly added to over the centuries.*

*Teatime. Kay is reunited with Maria Jones, thirteen
going on twenty-five, and her brother Peter, twelve,
going on fifty-five.*

Maria A Punch and Judy man? *A Punch and Judy man?*
It's over a year since I've seen you, Kay Harker, and
you're still a total ass. Why on earth didn't you just ask
him to give his show here?

Kay I'm sorry, Maria, I didn't think of that. It was all
so confusing. He said I had to stop some wolves, as
Christmas depends on it. What do you think he meant?

Maria That modern advertising leaves a great deal to be
desired . . . He was trying to get you to hire him for his
show, don't you see?

Peter I can't say that Caroline Louisa would approve,
Maria. Where would he do it?

Maria We could put him in the study. There's nothing to
do there apart from read . . . Oh I know! We could
invite him over for our Robber Tea.

Kay Please, Maria, what's Robber Tea?

Maria give a snort of contempt.

Sorry, it's just I never heard it before . . .

Maria Oh, do stop saying please and apologising all the
time, you're worse than my mother! Isn't it perfectly
obvious? Robber Tea is a Jones family Christmas
tradition. Each year on this day, we make a campfire

inside, toast sausages and pretend we are highwaymen lying in wait on the moors.

Peter Well, I think it is very childish, if you don't mind me saying so.

Maria Oh Peter! If you weren't my brother, I would have to pop an orange in your mouth every time you opened it, you marvellous bore.

Peter I wish you would be civil to me for once.

Maria I wish that we could hear about a gang of jewel thieves in the neighbourhood, who have come down to burgle us while we are having our Christmas lunch! But we are ready waiting for them – and there is the most glorious gunfight!

Peter (*glumly*) I don't want guns for Christmas. I want plum pudding and a posset before bed.

Maria I only want a posset if there is a lot of brandy in it, or at the very least sherry.

The others look at her in amazement.

What? Christmas ought to be brought up to date. It ought to have gangsters, and aeroplanes and a *lot* of machine guns.

She points a toy tommy gun at Kay.

Your money or your life!

Kay (*hands in the air, only half playing*) I told you, I've lost all my money.

Maria jabs the gun at his chest.

Very well, will you settle for a Punch and Judy show?

Maria If you can find the old man. But be quick!

Kay I'd better ask Caroline Louisa first –

Maria aims the gun again.

I'll walk into town, then, and see if I can find him. He said he would be at The Drop of Dew.

Maria No doubt the roughest inn there is! The kind full of cut-throats and smugglers. That's where his sort hang out.

Peter Are you sure you want to go out in this weather? Look. It's started to snow.

So it has.

Kay (*wistful*) Perhaps there will be enough to make a snowman tomorrow.

Peter I don't like building snowmen. Your hands get frostbite and they always melt in the end.

Maria You are too dull for Christmas! The sentence is death!

Maria chases Peter off with her gun.
Kay sits and watches the snow alone for a moment, lost in thought.
Caroline Louisa enters with a lamp.

Caroline Kay! You gave me quite a fright, sitting alone there in the dark.

Kay I thought I might walk down to Condicote.

Caroline At this time of day? Whatever for?

Kay I thought that I would . . . go to the baker's for some muffins! If we're having buttered eggs.

Caroline You are such a darling. Very well – in that case, while you're there you might as well ask for an extra plum pudding . . .

Kay I will. Only you'll have to lend me some tin now my wallet is gone. I haven't a tosser to my kick.

Caroline Louisa lends him some money, and he is off.

Caroline . . . And don't be late! I want us to sit down all together for tea . . . (*He's gone.*) Like we're a real family.

Caroline Louisa is alone, and as Seekings melts away, she looks out at the falling snow, and sings as Kay makes his way through the town to the pub.

Caroline
In the bleak midwinter
   Frosty wind made moan,
Earth stood hard as iron,
   Water like a stone;
Snow had fallen, snow on snow,
   Snow on snow,
In the bleak midwinter
   Long ago.

A suggestion of Kay's snowy and perilous hike to a pub at the wrong end of town.
   Glimpses of old market stalls, hanging butcher's carcasses, grinning masks in toyshop windows, a flash of gold from a ring . . . .
   And voices, gathering in the dark, whispering . . .

'The wolves are running.'
'If you see someone, say someone's safe.'

FIVE
THE DROP OF DEW

The voices are drowned out by wolves faintly howling in the dark, a battered pub sign creaking.
   Cole sits in a corner by a fire, polishing a small box, Toby at his feet.

Kay (*slowly approaching Cole*) Please, sir, what do you mean by 'wolves'?

Cole You will find that when the wolves are abroad, they take many forms.

Kay Mr Hawlings, my friends, they asked me –

Cole – would I go up to Seekings with my Punch and Judy show?

Kay Please, sir, how did you know what I was going to say?

Cole It is of no matter. But I will be there.

Kay Thank you. It will make their Christmas. Are you . . . very expensive?

Cole How if I was to say a biscuit for Toby, and a dish of eggs and bacon for me?

Kay I'm sure we can manage that!

Cole Now, seeing as you have rumpaged all the way here, I have something special to show you.

He sets the Box on the table.

This is what those wolves are after. It is my Box of Delights.

Kay Sorry, we haven't done that at school yet.

Cole It is not taught in schools, and nor will it ever be.

Kay Oh. What does it do?

Cole It does a great many things. But first, tell me what you would most like to see in the world?

Kay I don't know . . .

Cole If you could see anything.

Kay The King of England and all his soldiers on parade?

Cole Come. Is that truly what you would most like to see in all the world?

Kay No . . . I suppose . . . I would like to see my mother and father again, more than anything.

Cole Why, when did you last see them?

Kay A long time ago . . . Six years ago this Christmas . . . There was a fire . . .

Cole Master Kay. The Box can do many things. But it cannot bring back the dead into the land of the living.

Kay Then what can it do?

Cole (*kindly*) Well now – is there anything that might remind you of them?

Kay I'm not sure . . . Yes, there was a brooch my mother always wore. It was destroyed in the fire. A golden Phoenix. But Phoenixes don't exist, either, do they?

Cole Ah, perhaps they do.

  He opens the Box.

Look at the desert sands, where the pebbles are diamonds . . .

  He reaches in, takes a handful of sand and scatters it over the fire.
  A luscious palm tree appears.

Look now, the spice tree, can you smell it?

  The leaves part to reveal a glittering Phoenix.

Kay A Phoenix! My mother used to tell me that they could sing. Do you think this one can?

  The Phoenix begins to sing, a haunting cry. As it sings, feathers slowly fall away. Then it bursts into flames, till only ash remains.

Cole Watch now. Still watch.

An egg rolls out from the ash. Kay takes it and watches a baby Phoenix hatch.

You see, Master Kay, nothing is ever truly gone. It is just reborn in another form, as is the way of things. Those that we love are taken from us time and time again. But look – the beauty of their memory never fades.

The baby Phoenix flies off. They watch after it for a moment.

Kay (*subdued*) It was just a trick, though, wasn't it?

Cole Master Kay, there are tricks, what court jesters are known for, and then there is magic . . . which can change the fate of the earth we stand upon. Magic of space and time. One is much harder and rarer than the other, which is why we must always beware those doing only tricks.

Kay (*realising*) The vicar on the train! I'm such a duffer!

Cole But come along now, the snow is deepening . . . so you shall see me at Seekings, with my Punch and Judy and my little dog Toby at one half after five . . . So, for now, Master Harker –

He taps the Box, and disappears, leaving Kay alone again. He wanders in the snow back to Seekings, as the company sing:.

Company
What can I give Him,
    Poor as I am?
If I were a shepherd
    I would bring a lamb,
If I were a wise man
    I would do my part,
Yet what I can I give Him,
    Give my heart.

A book- and painting-lined study with French windows.
Peter drapes a rug over some chairs to make a den.
Maria and Kay huddle under it with him as they enjoy a
'Robber Tea' of sausages and toast.

Maria Well, you have earned your Robber Tea all right.
I'm almost jealous.

Peter You wouldn't catch me out in the snow on a wild
goose chase after some man you met on a train.

Kay It was strange. No one else seemed to have seen
Mr Hawlings. I feel like I'm making him up sometimes.

Peter Do you do that a lot?

Kay What?

Peter Make things up.

Kay Well, people at school say I do.

Peter I wish I could make things up.

Maria Poor Peter doesn't even know how to make a joke.

Peter You don't seriously think your tramp is a
magician, do you, Kay?

The French windows blow open in a gust of snow.
Kay runs up to close it . . . but there is Cole,
struggling in, with his case and Toby.

Kay Mr Hawlings!

Cole It is a wild night, Master Harker, as wild as any
I've known – and I've been a long time on the roads.

Maria (*suspicious*) How long?

Cole Well, first there were pagan times, then there were in-between times, then there were Christian times, and pudding time – but the times I liked best were the in-between times.

Maria Well, you might also know this time as teatime. *Robber* teatime – and I for one am jolly hungry for our show!

Peter I am so sorry about my sister, sir. She is quite the rudest member of my entire family. Can I offer you a cup of tea?

Cole Don't you worry, Master Peter. Now . . . young Miss Maria, being so bright as you are, can you tell me, does a travelling man collect as he goes, or doesn't he?

Maria He does.

Cole He does, she says. He collects, and what he collects . . . he shows!

Cole sets up his Punch and Judy 'theatre' with a flourish. Out tumble three glowing balls, which Cole juggles and then throws to the children one by one. As they catch the balls, they split open like eggs to reveal:
A toy mouse for Peter.
A paper butterfly for Kay.
And a red rose for Maria.

These are all little things, which a travelling man collects as he goes. And now I'll show you a play.

He prepares to perform.

Maria Is this the Punch and Judy show at last? I want to see a baby get biffed on the nose.

Cole (*behind box*) It is a kind of Punch and Judy show, Miss Maria, but the kind from olden times, from where I do hail.

He acts out his story with shadow puppets as he talks. Music.

Once, long ago, there was a great philosopher, and his name was Ramon Lully.

Ramon appears, a wise old elder with a beard and a tiny puppet dog.

Maria (*disappointed*) A philosopher! I want more magic.

Kay I think 'philosopher' is just an old-fashioned word for magician.

Cole Indeed. Ramon was famous throughout the land for his magical gifts. Yet he had a rival.

Arnold appears, sharp and sly.

Arnold of Todi. A sorcerer so powerful, that no one could say who was the greatest of them both. There was only one way to decide.

Maria A knife fight to the death!

Peter I would ask a Professor to make an empirical judgement based on the historical evidence available.

Kay Shh!

Cole They made a wager with each other. To see who between them could first come up with a piece of magic so incredible that it had never been done before.

Peter I'd like to see the trains run on time at Christmas. That has never been done before.

Maria I'd like to see a tale *about* a woman told *by* a woman, that would shake things up.

Ramon and Arnold shake hands.

Cole Ramon and Arnold went away for a year and a day. Then, at Christmas, Ramon reappeared with an

Elixir of Eternal Life. Anyone who drank it would live forever!

We see Ramon brandishing a vial.

Kay Surely that meant he won the bet?

Cole But then, Arnold of Todi returned, with a magic box of his own construction. A box of many delights, the greatest of which was the ability to travel through time.

Arnold reappears with a box.

Kay The Box of Delights!

Maria So go on then – who won?

Cole There was no winner, Miss Maria. For the very next day, Arnold of Todi disappeared, taking his Box with him. And he has not been seen since, until . . .

He is interrupted by Carol Singers, heard through the windows, singing 'First Noël'.

Carol Singers
They looked up and saw a star
Shining in the East beyond them far
And to the earth it gave great light
And so it continued both day and night.
Noël, Noël, Noël, Noël
Born is the King of Israel!

Peter (*running to window*) Carol singers!

Cole begins quietly packing up.

And look, they've got Japanese lanterns!

Maria How ghastly. Shall I rush upstairs and tip a cauldron of boiling oil over them?

Caroline (*entering*) I'd rather if you didn't Maria – it's the Cathedral Choir from Tatchester, including the Bishop himself.

Kay Caroline Louisa, this is Mr Hawlings, the Punch and Judy man I told you about. He's just given us a brilliant show about a magic box. Can we give him some bacon and eggs?

But Cole has disappeared again.

Caroline Yes, dear, very amusing. Now dressing-up time is over. Come along, tidy up!

Maria But it's *Robber Tea*.

Caroline Yes, and now we are having *grown-up* tea – with the Bishop of Tatchester. I need you to help hand around the muffins and cocoa. Quick march please!

The Carol Singers – including the Bishop – enter with their lanterns, singing full voice now.

Carol Singers
Then entered in those Wise Men three
Full reverently upon their knee
And offered there in His presence
Their gold and myrrh and frankincense.
Noël, Noël, Noël, Noël
Born is the King of Israel!

SEVEN
SEEKINGS STUDY, A LITTLE LATER

The Carol Singers finish and part to reveal Caroline Louisa and the children watching the Bishop drain his cocoa. Caroline Louisa a model of politeness.

Bishop And now, dear lady, I fear we must conclude this happy tour, and make our way back.

Bishop makes to go, Singers following.

But before I do, I must return your kind hospitality.

Tomorrow night, we are having a children's party, with games, five o'clock at the Bishop's Palace – and you are all invited!

Peter Even Maria?

Bishop Yes, Peter, especially my friend little Maria.

Maria Even though last year I started your car and drove it into a lamp post?

Bishop Christmas is a time for forgiveness, my dear . . .

Puts on coat, scarf, about to depart.

Caroline A party, though, Maria – aren't we lucky?

Maria The only parties I like are the kind that happen in dark basements with jazz music and men wearing make-up.

Caroline Your Grace, let me show you to your car.

As the Bishop follows Caroline out, Cole is at the door, with Toby.

Kay The Punch and Judy man! Look, Caroline Louisa! He *is* real.

But she's left already.

Perhaps he's forgotten something.

Bishop Ah, Mr Hawlings. We have met before, I think.

Cole You've seen me many a time, Your Grace.

Old friends – looks exchanged.

Bishop And very glad to have seen you now – it's given me an idea. Will you put on a special festive show for the children at our party tomorrow night?

Cole Indeed, I shall – for I have played a Christmas play on that night ever since pagan times.

Bishop Thank you – we shall expect you at the Bishop's Palace at half past four tomorrow. And now I really must bid you all goodnight!

The Bishop and Singers depart.

Kay (*to Cole*) You came back. Caroline Louisa didn't even believe you were real. I thought you'd left us.

Cole That I had to, Master Kay . . . If you would but close your eyes and listen a moment, you will hear why.

A wolf howls ominously in the distance.

Peter Someone must have let their dog out.

Kay That isn't a dog, Peter, it's a wolf.

Maria Nobody move! I'm going to fetch my pirate costume. That will scare off any wolf.

Cole It is the snow that brings the wolves out. Many a bitter night did we see them off before, but now here, once more, they're running, in many forms. We must stand to our spears.

Maria Spears! That is the best idea anyone has had all day. There is a curtain pole in our bedroom – come on, Peter, let's go and make ourselves a spear or two.

Peter Can't I just stay and have another muffin?

Maria No!

Maria drags Peter off.
Just Cole and Kay now.
We hear there is a pack of wolves, drawing closer.

Cole The pack has surrounded us, as wolves are wont to do. They must not find me.

Cole moves to the front door, but Toby growls excitably.
Lights flicker.

Kay We could hide in the study – or upstairs, under my bed?

Scratching noises at the door.
The lights go out.

Cole (*lighting a match*) There is no more time for hiding, Master Harker. The wolves are running after me, and they've run me close this time.

Kay Why do they want you so badly?

Cole It's not me, it's my Box of Delights. That which I showed you at the inn.

The French windows shake violently, as if something is trying to get in, something of supernatural force and energy.
Toby suddenly growls like a much bigger dog, at the windows, holding them off for a moment.
Cole produces the Box of Delights.

If I hand that to you, Master Harker, will you keep it safe for me?

Kay Shouldn't you go to the police?

Wolves outside catch the scent – whining for it.

Cole The police cannot stop these wolves. For this Box does not belong to me. It belongs to –

Kay Arnold of Todi! The sorcerer in your play.

Cole The very same, Master Harker. He goes a long way back, almost as long as me.

Kay How did you get hold of it?

Cole It shames me – but I played a trick, at a fair.

Kay You stole it off him!

Cole He could have done so much good with this Box, and instead all he wants is harm.

Kay Why, what can it do?

Cole It can do three things.

He gives Kay the Box. The Box shudders, with a glow and creepy hum.

This Box is full of old magic, Master Harker. It carries the weight of ages past, and burns with the desire of those who would seek to possess its delights. You must handle it with great care . . . Here's the first thing. You see this lever? If you push it to the right, you can go as small as a mouse. Now, the second. If you press it to the left, you can go as swift as a falcon.

Kay What's the third thing?

Cole The third thing . . . is the most powerful delight of the Box, but also the most dangerous, Master Harker.

A pane of glass smashes, a clawed paw thrusts through, trying to grasp the handle.
Cole looks around, cornered.

Quick. Tell me – what is that picture, there?

Kay It's of Bottler's Down, just outside Condicote. My father painted it. It's the only thing of his I could save from the fire.

Cole Bottler's Down . . . A picture you love, and know well?

Kay nods.

And now you look at it afresh, with your young eyes, do you perhaps see something new?

As Kay looks at the painting, it starts to glow and shimmer.

Cole and Toby step into the painting and vanish.

(*Offstage.*) Look after the Box, Master Harker! Guard it with your life. Christmas depends upon it.

Kay With my life? Mr Hawlings! Come back!

The French windows are flung open.
And the wolves have become Charles and Pouncer, disguised as Carol Singers with lanterns.

Charles What ho, Bishop! Are we too late for the concert, ha-ha what?

Pouncer sniffs the painting with suspicion.

Kay (*coldly*) Yes. I think you'll find the Bishop has already left. (*He points to the door.*) *That* way.

Pouncer How unfortunate . . . and it is so terribly cold outside. You wouldn't want us to catch a chill now, would you?

Kay You stole my wallet on the train. I think you should go.

Pouncer It sounds like there has been the most awkward misunderstanding. We were only hoping to catch up with your Punch and Judy man.

Kay He's gone and you aren't going to find him.

Charles Oh, aren't we? We'll have to see about that, ha-ha what . . .

Charles and Pouncer lay hands on Kay, just as Maria and Peter return.
Maria is dressed as a terrifying Blackbeard character – a beard, covered in knives, huge boots.
She pulls along Peter in an ill-fitting Smee costume on a leash.

Pouncer And who do we have here? What an enchanting beard, little girl. I have never seen one so . . . fiery . . . before.

Maria I'm sorry, but we are playing pirates now, and you're not invited, so you have to leave. Goodbye.

Charles But –

Maria throws one of her knives into the door frame by his head. The intruders do not need much more persuading as she escorts them out.

Peter Maria! You are so rude. They were carol singers from the Cathedral. What will the Bishop think?

Kay No, Peter, they weren't carol singers. They were thieves. Or wolves . . . I think they want to do something bad to Mr Hawlings.

Maria (*yelling out of the door*) Come back! Come back! I challenge you to a cutlass duel! To the death!

Caroline Louisa returns.

Caroline Darlings – what on earth is going on? Dear Maria, how many times have I told you not to play with the kitchen knives? The poor cook will never speak to me again.

Kay Caroline Louisa! You're back! We've been so scared. First there were wolves outside, and then those pickpockets from the train broke in, looking for Mr Hawlings, but he escaped through a painting – where have you been?

Caroline My dearest Kay, I can't take any of that in, I'm afraid. I've had the most awful news.

Caroline Louisa stumbles. Kay steadies her.

Kay What? What is it?

Caroline One of the carol singers, a most charming cleric, said there was a telegram for me at the Crown Hotel, and . . .

Maria (*thrilled*) Are we at war?

Caroline No, Maria! It's my brother. He has suddenly been taken very ill. It's all very mysterious. I must go and see him. I'm taking the last train up tonight. I'm sorry.

Kay But that means –

Caroline Yes, Kay, I am afraid it means that I won't be here for the first night of the holidays.

Kay You're leaving us on our own. Again.

Caroline Don't torment me! I'll be back tomorrow . . . or as soon as I can. I'm sure you'll manage. You always do. And if you can't, you know Ellen the maid is always here. So be good children, I'll be back for Christmas, I hope . . .

She sees their faces.

I promise!

Caroline kisses Kay and leaves. For a moment, the children are disconcerted and abandoned.

Peter I suppose . . . does that mean I can go early up the stairs to Bedfordshire with my book? It's on naval history.

Maria Don't you see? Now Caroline Louisa has gone, we can have a proper adventure at last. One with *real* blood. Shall we go and rough up some vicars, Kay?

Kay No . . . Look – (*He points to the floor.*) Those people who broke in just now. They were on foot, in the snow.

Peter I hope they were wearing sensible footwear.

Kay If the wolves are after us, then we shall be like wolves too . . . and track their footprints.

He puts his coat on and steps through the windows.

Maria This is going to be the best Christmas ever!

Peter Going out in the snow *again*?

Kay Yes, and going out alone. I promised Mr Hawlings I would keep his Box safe.

Maria Don't you dare –

Kay Let me find out more first, Maria, and then I promise you all the swordfights in the world.

Maria If I had a penny for every time that promise had been made . . . Well, go if you must, but if I am on a steamer to Argentina with a rich and handsome explorer by the time you return, don't blame me.

She drags Peter off. Kay is left alone. He takes the Box out.

Kay Now, what did the old man say? Press to the right to go –

He shrinks to Tiny Kay.

Oh! As small as a mouse! It works!

Tiny Kay scurries off as Seekings falls away, the Carol Singers departing faintly in the background.

Company
  The holly and the ivy,
  When they are both full grown,
  Of all the trees that are in the wood,
  The holly bears the crown.

The rising of the sun
And the running of the deer,
The playing of the merry organ,
Sweet singing in the choir.

EIGHT
MONK'S PIECE

*A holly-and-ivy clad fragment of a ruined gothic
monastery on the edge of Condicote. Charles and
Pouncer creep in, flashing their torches.*

Pouncer Where has the old fool got to this time?

Charles nervously lights his pipe.

Charles Careful, my dear, we don't know who may be
listening. Are you there, ha-ha what?

Abner (*singing, deadly*)
Long, long ago
Or did Now happen a long time ago?
Long, long ago . . .

Charles He's coming!

*Abner approaches through the dappled shadows of
the old cloister.*

Abner (*bowing*) Charles. (*Offering his hand.*) Pouncer,
my Queen of the Night.

Pouncer My Lord of Darkness, my Abner.

Abner So! You missed the old man. For the second time.

Charles He must have been among the Bishop's Choir
and we never noticed, ha-ha what?

Abner Do you ever notice anything, I wonder, Charles?
My Pouncer here assured me you were the best at

43

scrobbling in all of London. You certainly cost a fair penny.

Pouncer He is a clever wretch. He used the old magic to outwit us in a way that not even you could have foreseen, my Omniscient One.

Abner Perhaps it seems so to you, my Prescient Puss. I would have thought it entirely obvious. Hawlings escaped you both on the train, and now he has again. I am losing my patience, and trust me, you do not want to see me lose my patience.

Charles You'd have thought him a carol singer, just as we did, ha-ha what? Very convincing costume, good singing voice . . .

His voice fades as he sees Abner's stony expression.

Abner Would I, Charles, my far-seeing friend? I wonder. Where is my Rat? Perhaps he can tell me something useful. Rat! Where are you, curse your rotten tail!

Splashes and snarls. A greasy and sinister Rat twitches into view.

Rat Down in the cellars and tunnels I run, all weathers, all hours – for one 'oo would sell his own mother, if 'e 'ad one, to be ground down into old bones.

Abner You are too kind. Now tell me what you know, Rat, before I grind *you* into old bones.

Rat Maybe I will, maybe I won't. 'Oo's the lovely lady?

Abner This, Rat, is my wife, Sylvia Daisy Pouncer, and you will do well to watch your words with her.

Rat Why, is she a witch?

Pouncer (*smiling sweetly*) Like you wouldn't believe. Now, tell us your news, unless you want to meet my black cat. He has rather a fondness for rats. Especially their eyes.

Rat What will I get for it? I could kill for a piece of green cheese.

Abner Here is some green cheese for you then.

Charles and Pouncer are revolted . . .

Rat Now, this is wot I call cheese . . . This would close any tavern down!

Abner Then jump to it. Tell me. What do you know about Hawlings and his Box? *My* Box!

Rat You will find 'im you seek at the place they call Bottler's Down.

Charles Bottler's Down? Impossible! He has gone to Tatchester, with the Bishop. We saw with our own eyes, ha-ha what?

Rat You asked me what I know, this is wot I know. I heard it all through the wainscoting. Do you have any more of that cheese?

Abner Very well! And will he have the . . . goods on him?

Rat That is a very good question. I'll ask again, do you have any more of that cheese?

Abner Silence, you repulsive rodent! I need that Box, by Christmas Eve. The thousandth Christmas at Tatchester Cathedral.

Rat For some bacon rind? It does make my fur shine so.

Abner For bacon rind!

Rat Then if you want that Box, I reckon you must scrobble 'im on Bottler's Down at dawn tomorrow.

Abner My Box! My precious Box of Delights. Soon it will be mine again. Charles, do you think you can follow a simple instruction this time?

Charles Scrobbling old men in the snow? I was rather hoping for a little more glamour, ha-ha what?

Abner I won't ask you again. Or do you want a little visit to the Scrounger?

Charles Rather not, thanks.

Abner Then how many times do I need to ask you? Get to Bottler's Down! Get!

Charles hurries off.

Rat One last thing though before I go . . .

Abner Yes, what is it? Come come, Rat!

Rat I definitely will have my bacon rind?

Abner Yes! You shall have three rancid kippers and a flaming haggis! My thundering sky, tell me!

Rat There is a boy, Kay Harker . . .

Abner Never mention that name again! Get back to your tunnel, you loathsome rodent. Or there will be no bacon rind, and no cheese, ever again!

Rat I was only telling you what I spied. The Rat don't like the boy neither . . . would give him a nip if I could . . .

Rat crawls out of sight, muttering to himself.

Abner Kay Harker! Again!

Pouncer I did tell you, my Wise One. Like a bad penny.

Abner Have no fear, my Radiance, our plans are too advanced now to fail. We can brook no interference from a meddling child.

Pouncer Shall I make a plan for him too?

Abner Yes, yes, you magical minx!

Abner and Pouncer disappear into the shadows. A tumble of stones as a watcher appears from his hiding place. Tiny Kay.

NINE
SEEKINGS, CHILDREN'S BEDROOM

Maria has tied Peter to a bedpost.

Peter Can't I go to bed, Maria? I ate too many muffins and I really could do with my book.

The window opens. Kay clambers in.

Where have you been so long? Maria has been torturing me all evening.

Maria We thought you had been abducted by a gang.

Peter You've got gangs on the brain, Maria.

Kay Those thieves are in a gang all right. And their leader is a strange devil in a silk dressing gown called Abner Brown. He knew my name. He seems familiar too somehow . . .

Peter A gang of thieves, in Condicote! Shouldn't we tell the police then?

Maria If you ever read a novel rather than dreary history books, you'd know that is the last thing we should do . . . So what *are* we going to do, Kay?

Kay Abner has sent his wolves to go and scrobble Mr Hawlings at Bottler's Down. We must try and stop them. Will you come with me?

Maria I'd rather do anything than go to bed.

Peter We'll catch our death of cold.

Kay Look, Peter. It's stopped snowing.

Peter But to go out in the middle of the night on the first day of the holidays – I think it's the Purple Pim, I truly do.

Kay Come on, we can forage in the larder first.

Peter Can we take some mince pies with us?

Kay As many as you can carry.

Peter Oh, all right then!

They set off into the snow, singing.

Children
It came upon the midnight clear,
That glorious song of old,
From angels bending near the earth,
To touch their harps of gold:
'Peace on the earth, goodwill to men,
From heaven's all-gracious King.'
The world in solemn stillness lay,
To hear the angels sing.

TEN
BOTTLER'S DOWN

Overcoat pockets stuffed with larder rations, Kay, Maria and Peter lie high up on Bottler's Down, looking out over the snow, peering through binoculars.
    They have been there a while.

Maria When are these scrobblers going to show, or your old man for that matter? I am getting very cold and very bored. In fact, I would almost rather be back in bed. I hope you are not just a big fibber.

Kay People say snow can be warm if you get into it.

Maria Yes, that's just the kind of thing people say.

Kay Well, I'm sure we'll be back home soon.

Peter Kay, do you think Caroline Louisa will be back home soon? In time for Christmas?

Kay I'm sure she will.

Peter Only I wouldn't want us to be on our own. Not for Christmas.

Kay I'm sure she won't leave us on our own, Peter, don't worry.

Maria I wish she would, then we could have even more adventures.

Peter Kay . . . Don't you ever miss your mother and father at Christmas?

Kay (*quiet*) I do. More than you can imagine. Every year.

Peter Yes, that must be rotten . . . Oh hang on! (*Focuses binoculars.*) What's that? I can see some animal tracks, over there in the snow.

Kay Wolves?

Peter No, of course not wolves. There aren't any left in England. But there are some fox tracks here . . . and rabbits . . .

Maria (*pointing*) But even better than all that, look over there.

Peter Footprints! The beginning of the trail is covered up by the fresh snow. And there . . . dog prints alongside. Your old man had a dog, didn't he, Kay? It must be him!

Kay (*following with binoculars*) It is. Look! (*He points.*)

The trail leads over that old wall . . . into that ditch . . . and through the wood.

Maria And there's your old man with his case all right. He can hardly carry it.

We see Cole struggling through the snow with Toby and his case . . . Charles and Pouncer sneak up, and place a sack over his head, dragging him off.

They're scrobbling him!

The children run over.

Peter Too late, they've bundled him into that car.

Kay They'll never get away in this snow, that will stick the moment they try to move.

Maria Come on then!

Kay Wait –

What sounds like an aeroplane nearby noisily prepares to take off, and then it does –
The children start back in alarm –
But this isn't a plane –
Or a bird –
Or a superhero –
But a modern technological wonder of fiendish wizardry – a flying car!
The car-o-plane soars up over their heads.

Peter I say, Kay, I am glad I came out with you after all. I never thought I should see a gang abduct an old man by putting a bag over his head and carrying him off in a car that turned into an aeroplane.

Maria Well what did you expect? Now come on!

Kay If we follow their tracks we might be able to get some evidence to take to the police . . .

They hurry after the trail, as the car-o-plane powers off into the night over our heads.

ELEVEN
CONDICOTE POLICE STATION

Wreathed in shadow, the Police Inspector looks down from a great and remote height over his counter at the children. He might as well be in another world.

Inspector So, you all just stood and watched as this old man was bundled into an aeroplane?

Kay It happened so quickly . . .

Inspector I suspect it was just some young officers from the aerodrome having a frolic. A bit of a Christmas gambol!

Maria But what about Mr Cole Hawlings, the Punch and Judy man? Where has he gone then?

Phone rings, Inspector answers.

Inspector Condicote 7000? Yes . . . Well, ha-ha what indeed . . . (*He puts his hand over the receiver.*) That is a most charming cleric at Tatchester now, just asking if I can give a licence to your Punch and Judy man, so as he can give a public performance at the Bishop's Palace this very afternoon.

Kay It can't be! Can I speak to him?

Inspector First, if you would be so kind, can you tell me if your Mr Hawlings is fit to perform for the Bishop?

Kay Of course, he's wonderful, but –

Inspector (*into phone*) Your Reverence, I have every reason to believe that this is a performer of good character who can be trusted not to shock or disappoint. Your licence is granted.

The Inspector hangs up.

Kay Which Reverend? Why couldn't we speak to Mr Hawlings?

Inspector He was called away, young Master Kay, before I could hand him on . . . He said he was expected at the Bishop's Palace most imminently and I did not want the Law to stand in the way of the Church, now, did I?

He marches off, whistling 'We Wish You a Merry Christmas'.

TWELVE
THE BOX OF DELIGHTS

The children are alone again.

Kay It was jolly odd that he didn't let me speak to Mr Hawlings.

Maria Well, come on then, Kay. You got us into this scrape. Where next? I can smell adventure.

Kay Before Mr Hawlings left Seekings, he gave me this box. I have to keep it safe for him, I promised on my life. It's the most special thing I've ever been given.

He produces the Box of Delights with a flourish.

Peter (*nonplussed*) It looks like one of Mama's old jewellery boxes.

Maria Or a buried treasure chest! What's inside?

Kay That's just it . . . I don't know exactly. Do you remember the play about the two philosophers?

Peter I remember . . . One was very good, and one was very rotten. And that the good one had a very scruffy beard, like an old sailor. The other didn't have a beard and was evil.

Kay Do you remember what the rotten one made to win his wager?

Maria (*excited*) Arnold of Todi's Box of Delights!

Kay Exactly. And I think this is it.

Peter I reckon that was just a silly yarn he told to keep us quiet.

Maria You would.

Kay It must be thousands of years old. This box is why they scrobbled him into that plane . . . why they robbed me on the train . . . and why the wolves are running.

Maria Well, go on then? What does it do, Mr Todi's precious box?

Kay He said that if I pushed the lever to go right, I would go small – and I do! And if I pushed to the left, I would go swift. But I haven't tried that yet . . .

Maria Never mind the lever . . . what's inside?

Kay He didn't say.

He hesitates.

Maria Go on! Maybe it's full of gold and diamonds, to make our fortune.

Kay I don't know . . . It's very precious and old. He's already shown me some of the magic . . . it's so powerful.

Maria Kay Harker. What is the point of having a Box of Delights if we can't delight in it? Open the Box!

Kay Very well. Perhaps if I press the switch down . . .

As he does, the Box begins to sparkle inside. A sound of birdsong.

Peter I do hope he hasn't trapped a canary in there. The Animal Welfare League will be on to us.

Maria Look! It's opening itself.

The Box opens slowly, light filling their faces from inside.

Kay sets the open Box down, as hawthorn trees emerge, creating an opening into a forest, sprinkling white blossom on the children.

Kay A forest! It's alive!

Animals appear – a shy deer, sleepy dormouse, eager rabbits, blackbirds – a mini-ballet.

The animals disappear back into the forest as a jingling sound approaches.

An ancient pagan face of bone and shadow looms out of the darkness in the woods.

Herne the Hunter!

Wearing antlers and many chains.

Herne Hello, Kay. Hello, children.

Maria My parents told me never to talk to strangers. *Especially* ones dressed like that. Who are you?

Herne I am Herne the Hunter. This box is made from my oak, and I remain its guardian. Welcome to my wild wood.

Maria You can't be much of a hunter. We've just been dive-bombed by every wild bird in Britain.

Herne Why don't you come in and take a closer look?

They follow Herne into the wood.

Kay This is so beautiful. I shall never know even a hundredth of all the things there are to know.

Herne You will do if you stay with me. Become a stag and discover for yourself . . .

Kay runs out from the wood as a stag that runs and jumps.

Kay It's so lovely to feel the grass beneath my feet!

Maria What do I get? The great failing of English woods, in my opinion, is their lack of tigers.

Herne I think for you, Miss Maria . . . how about a wild duck?

Maria (*groans*) If you must . . . as long as I don't have to go anywhere near the water . . . Ooh!

Maria emerges as a duck, that soars high, honking.

Everything looks so little and far away . . . this is too much fun!

Peter (*depressed*) I suppose I'm going to have to become an animal now too, aren't I?

Herne Yes, you are, Peter. To see the world through new eyes.

Peter And what have you chosen for me? A falcon, perhaps? Or a cunning fox?

Herne No. A trout.

Peter appears as a trout, unhappy.

Peter But how beautiful and fresh the water is!

Even Peter gets into the spirit. All three children and their animals thrill to their new sense of being.

Kay I could be a deer forever!

Maria And I a duck!

Peter Not entirely sure about this trout business.

Herne Be careful though, children . . . I told you the wood was wild.

The mood darkens.

Kay What is it? What's happening now?

Herne Watch out for the wolves in the wood, Kay.

A wolf with glowing eyes appears.

And for the hawks in the sky, Maria.

Maria gives a cry of alarm as a sharp-beaked hawk dives after her.

Peter Ha! A hawk can't catch me!

Herne Beware the pike in the reeds, Peter!

A huge dark pike closes in on Peter.

They have taken Cole, they will take others; but don't lose courage, Kay. You will beat the wolves, won't you, Kay?

Kay manages to snap the Box shut.
    Herne, light, trees and animals all vanish. It takes a moment for it to sink in.

Maria No wonder your old man treasured this Box. Why do you think this Abner Brown wants it so badly?

Kay Don't you see? Because he could go anywhere he wished . . . back in time, forward in time . . . as any person or creature that ever existed.

Maria He could do anything he wanted!

A moment as the children's excitement turns to awe and fear of the Box.

Peter Well . . . magic box or no magic box, I for one know where I would like to visit next.

Maria Please don't say, 'Up the stairs to Bedfordshire.'

Peter I've had quite enough adventure for one day. And I would like to go up the stairs –

Maria Preserve me. He's saying it –

Peter – to Bedfordshire!

Kay Perhaps if we ask her nicely, Ellen will even make us a hot posset?

Maria *and* **Peter** Now you're talking!

Kay In that case, let's see if the other lever does as promised. Everyone hold on tight. Ready? Box . . . go swift . . . straight to Seekings!

The children and Box vanish swiftly.

THIRTEEN
THE CELLARS

A dank and dark sewery place.

Abner (*offstage*)
Long, long ago
Or did Now happen a long time ago?
Long, long ago . . .

Abner appears with Pouncer.

Rat? Where are you, you rascally rodent?

Rat appears again, chewing and twitching.

Pouncer (*holding her nose*) Well, what have you got for us this time?

Rat What have you got for *me* . . .

Abner (*sighs*) What do you want?

57

Rat It's only, I can't stand the climate like I used to . . . I know it's poison, but . . .

Abner Pouncer, my most Queenly Quartermaster, a tot of rum for this Rat.

Reluctantly, Pouncer produces a hip-flask and pours Rat a thimble of rum.

Rat (*downing it*) Happy days! Ooh . . . I love a nice bit of poison I do!

Abner So, Rat, I ask you again. What have you got?

Rat My nephews and I tortured the old man wot you scrobbled.

Abner That's what I asked you to do, you wretched vermin. What have you got for me?

Rat splutters.

Abner Speak up! What have you got for me?

Rat Was I meant to do anything else?

Abner Nothing much . . . maybe just get me a fur hat for Pouncer here, a plum pudding for Charles . . . and my BOX! The Box I sent you to get.

Rat We searched your old man from the top of 'is head to the bottom of 'is boots but no Box thing did we find!

Abner Then I shall hang you! I shall hang you, by your tail, till your eyes fall out of your skull! Until you find me that Box!

Rat squeaks with fear and indignation.

Pouncer Too late to cry over spilt milk, my Brightness.

Abner But not too late to make the spiller cry, my Astuteness.

He puts on a pair of sinister gloves and grabs Rat by the throat.

You must have learned something from the old man. Tell me!

Rat Begging your mercy, but maybe he gave it to the boy – Kay Harker?

Abner I'm sorry, did you say something?

Rat Yes –

Abner strangles Rat to death, it is a shocking, painful and vicious moment.

Abner I didn't think so. (*To Pouncer.*) You see, my Opulent Opal, there is not a moment to lose. Find Charles. There must not be a stone unturned. Search Seekings. Churn up Condicote and turn over Tatchester.

Pouncer Even the Cathedral and the Bishop's Palace, my Saintliness?

Abner Especially the Bishop's Palace! Hawlings might have slipped him the Box during the carols. Scrobble who you have to. Steal what you must. But find me my Box of Delights before Christmas, my Puss, I beg of you.

Pouncer I feel, too late, my Sphinx, that we should not have trusted to this vermin. Perhaps we should just divide the jewels we have stolen, and not worry about this Box a moment longer . . .

Abner Impossible! That wretched Cole Hawlings may have given the Box to anyone. The Inspector of Police! The Bishop of Tatchester! The King of England!

Pouncer What a Shakespearean imagination you have, my Dove.

Abner Well, my Empress, any better ideas? There will be no diamonds for anyone, unless I have my Box.

Pouncer In that case, may a weak and feeble woman make a suggestion, my warlike one? Is it not possible that there may be some truth in what this creature said? (*She points to the dead Rat.*) Perhaps Hawlings may have entrusted this precious box of yours to one of the children?

Abner Kay Harker! No! Never! I can't believe that name would come to haunt me again . . . I hope you don't think, my Ideal, that he would have entrusted a treasure so great to a child he had not seen before yesterday afternoon?

Pouncer No, my Topaz and Diamond, not that dreamy little muff. But perhaps one of the other children there?

Abner Who?

Pouncer That sharp little girl who showed Charles and I the door so rudely. She looked most promising. Miss Maria. A girl who knows how to wear a fake beard and throw a knife.

Abner Do you think she might be hiding something?

Pouncer I know it. I recognise a kindred spirit.

Abner Do I see a plan forming, my Priceless Pearl?

Pouncer A plan of perfection, my dear Abbey.

Abner (*embracing her*) My Blue and Yellow Sapphire! My Emerald! My Ruby!

> *Abner and Pouncer waltz off through the mist, humming 'Long Long Ago' as Maria saunters on.*

Maria is getting ready for the party. She lays out a handkerchief. She takes out her pistol, and disassembles it on the handkerchief, then reassembles it, fast. She checks her watch, and repeats the process, faster.

Pouncer joins her, in disguise.

Pouncer Miss Maria Jones?

Maria (*distracted*) What does it look like?

Pouncer I don't know . . . what are you doing?

Maria I'm seeing how fast I can take apart and reassemble my pistol.

Pouncer Why on earth would a little girl be doing such a thing on the day before Christmas Eve?

Maria Isn't it obvious? I'm going to a party at the Bishop's. I need to be prepared.

Pouncer Which brings me to my reason for seeking you out. My name is Mrs Brown.

Maria Well do spit it out, Mrs Brown. (*Checks her watch again.*) There's a car taking us to Tatchester for the party, it will be here any minute.

Pouncer That's just it, Miss Maria, I come with a message from the Bishop himself.

Maria points her pistol at Pouncer.

Not *that* kind of message.

Maria What does he want? If he thinks I'm paying for the damage to his silly old motor car, he can try coming back next Christmas. And the one after that.

Pouncer As a matter of fact, he wondered whether you might like to come on a special tour of the stained glass at St Griswold's, and then back for tea at the Cathedral?

Maria It's a rather mouldy lot of glass at St Griswold's, isn't it?

Pouncer Yes . . . in the main church. But in the side chapel, there is some of the best that there was ever done.

Maria I don't know. It's pretty mouldy, all round, English glass, if you ask me.

Pouncer (*boiling point*) Well, I think you will find this isn't English glass!

Maria I might need more persuasion than that.

Pouncer We can offer you a light lunch at the Bear's Paw – their duck patty is highly regarded.

Maria is still not impressed.

Look . . . I fear I may have got off on the wrong foot. May I speak plainly?

Maria I do not know any other way.

Pouncer I thought as much. You see, Miss Maria, I think we have more in common than it may appear. To be frank, I too do not share the Bishop's enthusiasm for the glass at St Griswold's. I agree with you wholeheartedly about the dismal state of English glass. And, like you, I never leave the house without my gun.

Maria Phooey! You dress like a duchess and talk like a nanny. I don't believe you're carrying so much as a sharpened knitting needle.

Pouncer Oh, don't you?

Maria No, I don't.

Pouncer I do so hate to disappoint one of such tender years, but I am neither a duchess or a nanny. And this is very much a gun.

She produces a large pearl-handled revolver from her bag.

It's very popular with the gangsters of Chicago, I'm told.

Maria Well!

Pouncer Are you shocked?

Maria No, I'm wondering why on earth you kept that hidden under your lace handkerchief while you prattled on about stained glass.

Pouncer Do you like my revolver then, Miss Maria?

Maria I want to fire it immediately. How many ruffians have you shot?

Pouncer I'm afraid I lost count after a hundred.

Maria Better and better! Please, Mrs Brown, may I take a closer look?

Pouncer (*holding gun back*) It's rather a large gun for such a little girl.

Maria I think you'll find it's what I do with it that counts.

Pouncer In that case, what do you say to a little competition?

Maria As a rule, I only like to enter competitions which I am guaranteed to win.

Pouncer Well, we shall see. I challenge you that I can take apart and reassemble my revolver quicker than you can your pistol.

Maria I doubt that very much. What are the terms?

Pouncer If you win, I shall leave you in peace. If I win, you must come with me to St Griswold's.

Maria Go on then.

Pouncer (*setting her watch*) On the count of three. One . . . two . . . three.

They go about disassembling and reassembling their guns. Pouncer beats Maria by a whisker.

I reluctantly submit that occasionally there is something to be gleaned from the experience of an older woman. That was very fast. Where did you learn to do that?

Pouncer I was raised by nuns. They were very keen on self-defence. So, dear child . . . will you come now?

Maria If I must.

Pouncer The Bishop will be thrilled! Do you want to leave word that you will set off early?

Maria They won't worry. They know I always have my pistol with me, and that I'm a dead shot with both hands.

Pouncer How you must enjoy the quiet atmosphere of school.

Maria School! They know better than to try that game on me. I've been expelled from three, and the headmistresses still swoon when they hear my name. I'm Maria Jones! And I don't think I will come with you after all!

Pouncer Indeed you are, my dove, and I am Sylvia Daisy Pouncer.

Pouncer shoves a sack over Maria's head, and scrobbles her off, leaving the pistol abandoned . . . which soon disappears under the onslaught of instruments, lights, laughter and –

Company
    O Christmas tree! O Christmas tree!
    Much pleasure thou can'st give me;
    O Christmas tree! O Christmas tree!
    Much pleasure thou can'st give me;
    How often has the Christmas tree
    Afforded me the greatest glee!
    O Christmas tree! O Christmas tree!
    Much pleasure thou can'st give me.

FIFTEEN
THE BISHOP'S PALACE

*A finely decorated Christmas tree, in a mound of
wrapped gifts.*

*The Bishop stands to address the assembled party of
the Duchess of Tatchester, clergy and children – all in
their party hats and masks.*

Bishop Ladies and gentlemen, boys and girls, and –
(*Bows.*) our guest of honour, the Duchess of Tatchester,
welcome to our little gathering. Marvellous to see so
many of you. Where you now stand, pilgrims have stood
for generations. In fact, tomorrow night, on Christmas
Eve, we will be celebrating a thousand years of Christmas
here at Tatchester! Our Midnight Mass will be the
thousandth celebration of Christmas in Tatchester
Cathedral. There has been a midnight service every
Christmas Eve since the cathedral was founded, and
we want this to be the most special and spectacular
Christmas ever!

    Everyone cheers.

But first, tonight, Mr Hawlings will present his famous
Punch and Judy show, just as his grandfather used to . . .
So, let us make merry. And we'll begin – with some
presents!

Parcels are passed around and presents unwrapped to music.

A whistle! A drum! A trumpet!.

A pistol to fire a cork and knock off the Bishop's mitre!

Peter This is what Christmas is all about, isn't it?

Kay I suppose so.

Peter (*opening a scarlet and white stocking to pull out a toy sleigh*) A sleigh . . . oh . . . and even better, it's full of chocolate creams!

Bishop Hello, Kay. I'm so sorry to hear Caroline Louisa couldn't make it. Do you think she will be back for Christmas?

Kay I hope so. She telephoned this morning, to say that she had been delayed one more night.

Bishop What a shame . . .

Hands him an extravagantly wrapped gift.

I know this time of year is always . . . a difficult one for you . . . We thought you might enjoy this wonder.

The party fades, as Kay unwraps his present.
He holds it up, marvelling – a beautiful toy ship, tall sails gleaming – a moment of joy.

Kay (*reading the inscription in awe*) 'Captain Kidd's Fancy'!

Peter (*downcast*) Chocolate creams.

Bishop (*holding machine-gun-shaped parcel*) And I got this for my young friend Maria, to show there were no hard feelings after last year's little mishap . . . Oh! Is she not with you?

Peter We thought she was playing next door.

Bishop I'm afraid I haven't seen her at all.

Kay But she was meant to take a car here earlier . . .

Bishop Not to worry, I'm sure she'll turn up. Now . . . how about a little dance everybody? And then we will go next door, where Mr Hawlings is going to present his show . . .

The dance begins.

Ah, Duchess! So glad you could make it. Excuse me, boys –

Bishop makes for a grand bewigged lady, as Rogers, the Bishop's butler, appears, with a phone on a salver.

Butler Master Jones? A telephone call for you.

Peter steps aside to take the call.
Charles appears, dancing towards Kay, who is on his own and defenceless.
Then he sees what could be Cole.

Kay Mr Hawlings, it's Kay Harker, can I just –

Hawlings is swept off in the dance, as the Bishop returns.

Your Grace!

Bishop Yes, what is it, my boy?

Kay (*pointing to Charles*) That man there, he's –

Bishop Ah yes, a visiting missionary, Brother Charles. Most charming. Would you like to meet him?

Kay No . . . we've already met.

Bishop (*not listening*) Oh, but you must! I'll go and fetch him now.

The Bishop goes after Charles, caught up in the dance. Peter returns.

Peter Kay – there's been a break-in at Seekings! They've turned the place upside down! And then there was the most awful noise and screaming while I was talking to Ellen. I fear she may have been scrobbled too.

Kay That's not all. Look who's over there! We have to find Mr Hawlings and get him out of here. Your Grace! If I could just ask you one thing –

Bishop What is it now, Kay?

Kay Please – can I talk to the Punch and Judy man?

Bishop Unfortunately not. He is too busy preparing his show.

Rogers returns, out of sorts.

Now what is it, Rogers?

Butler It's a disaster! While the party has been going on – the entire place has been burgled!

Bishop At Christmas? The monsters. What have they taken?

Butler They've turned the place topsy-turvy – and taken everything! Even the Duchess's jewellery . . .

Bishop The heathens! I'm sorry, children, you'll have to excuse me. Rogers, you call the police, I'll break the news to the Duchess.

*The Bishop is seen being grave with the Duchess.
    Kay has spotted Cole and Toby, but can't get to
him through the masked dancers.*

Kay Look! Toby! Mr Hawlings!

Kay heads towards Cole.

Duchess (*screams*) My diamonds! My diamonds! My pearls!

Duchess runs off in distress.

Kay (*to Peter*) Do you think that old man is Mr Hawlings? If I could just get his attention . . . we could ask him what to do. Mr Hawlings!

The party breaks up in chaos, but one guest turns around to the children – Herne the Hunter, shining.

Herne They have taken Cole; they have taken Maria and Caroline Louisa. They will take others. But don't lose courage, Kay, even if the wolves are running.

Cole dances towards them, backwards. Everything now nightmarish and slow.

Kay I will try . . . Oh, he hasn't been scrobbled at all. There he is. Mr Hawlings! Mr Hawlings!

Kay finally catches up with Cole.
    Cole turns around – a wolf! Then Charles finally reaches them.

I'll use the Box.

He gets it out.

Charles The Box! I've got you now, ha-ha what!

Peter There isn't time, Kay – run!

Kay presses the Box and he and Peter vanish, pursued by Charles and the wolf.

SIXTEEN
THE CELLARS

Maria sits alone.
    A metal shutter is dragged open high above, revealing Pouncer.

Pouncer Good evening, Maria Jones.

Maria *Miss* Maria to you!

Pouncer My apologies. Good evening *Miss* Maria Jones. I hope we haven't inconvenienced you.

Maria Not in the least. That stained glass would have been mouldy anyway.

Pouncer There is no need to be afraid.

Maria I'm never afraid.

Pouncer I am glad to hear that. Please believe me that I speak the truth, when I say I admire so much courage in one so young.

Maria I shan't believe a word you ever say again! Raised by nuns! By wolves, more like.

Pouncer How very perceptive, Miss Maria. I see in you a kindred spirit. A dashing, fearless adventurer that I greatly desire as a young associate to join me and my colleagues.

Maria Are you a gang of crooks?

Pouncer No, we merely have . . . an ongoing business concern.

Maria What kind of business?

Pouncer Fighting injustice wherever we find it, that kind of thing.

Maria How do you do that?

Pouncer We can't possibly give away our methods to the uninitiated.

Maria Why do you want me, though? There must be more to it than a liking for stained glass and revolvers.

Pouncer There is! It's an awfully fun job for the young. Lots of motor cars, aeroplanes – life is one long mad social whirl!

Maria But what is the work exactly?

Pouncer *As I said*, we shall tell you once you join us.

Maria It can't be honest work, then. If it was, you would tell me.

Pouncer It's nice work, I promise you.

Maria It can't be nice, or you wouldn't be doing it.

Pouncer If children are pert here, we make them into dog biscuit!

Another shutter is dragged open. There is Abner.

Abner Ladies, ladies! The first word in business is unity. Let us have unity or we shall get nowhere. Miss Jones, do we have unity from you?

Maria Never!

Abner Very well. Then we shall have information instead!

Abner enters. Maria shrinks back.

We have a friend in common, a Punch and Judy Man, Mr Cole Hawlings.

Maria Yes, he put on a very strange show.

Abner But did he give you, or any of your companions, a small shiny Box?

Maria No . . .

Abner Wrong answer!

Abner puts on his sinister gloves and makes Maria cry out in pain.

Abner Next wrong answer, it will be worse . . . Did he leave the Box anywhere at Seekings?

Maria I don't know anything about a stupid Box of Delights.

Abner gives a sharp twist. Another cry.

Abner A Box of Delights? I don't believe I called it that. Do you, my shining star?

Pouncer I don't recall that you did, my Lion.

Maria Mr Hawlings mentioned something in his show. I don't know anything about it!

Abner The problem is, young Maria, is that we believe you do.

Pouncer And we have all the time in the world.

Abner We will see if a further spell in the dark cannot persuade you. If not, then there is always . . .

Pouncer The Scrounger!

Both Abner and Pouncer laugh, as the shutters noisily descend, drowning out Maria's screams.

SEVENTEEN
CHESTER HILLS

The creepy edge of a deserted wood, in a grey dawn. An old iron gate, chained.
   Lopsided signs on dark trees:
MISSIONARY COLLEGE
TRESPASSERS WILL BE PROSECUTED
Kay with his box and ship – and Peter with his chocolate creams – run on, breathless, covered in mud and snow.

Peter Do you think we've shaken him off?

Kay For now, it looks like it.

They collapse under a tree.

You see – the Box wasn't that bad.

Peter I'm sorry. It's just, I find it a bit . . .

Kay Frightening? I know, I do too. But is it any more frightening than those wolves?

Peter I just don't like going swift through the air at the touch of a button. I don't like to do anything swift as a rule, apart from eating chocolate creams.

Kay I don't like this any more than you do Peter.

A pause while Peter eats another chocolate cream and considers this.

Peter Kay . . . I know we're not related . . .

Kay What does it matter if we are or not?

Peter Well, I just wanted to say, that if a chap was going to have a brother . . .

Kay You've got a pretty brave sister, that's for sure. Who I'm sure we'll find again very soon.

Peter I know. But if I was to have a brother as well, I think you'd be a very solid one.

Kay Thank you Peter, you too.

Another chocolate cream . . .

Peter Kay?

Kay Yes, Peter?

Peter Do you think I'm the most tremendous plank?

Kay (*hiding it*) No, not at all . . . not the *most* tremendous plank, by any means.

Peter But you do still think I'm a plank? I knew it. That's what everyone at school thinks too. Peter the Plank, they call me.

Kay That's not what I meant – I say, where are we? (*Looking around.*) I think the Box has brought us all the way to Hope-le-Chesters. Look – the Missionary College! That's where the couple who robbed me on the train were headed to!

Peter So what if it is?

Kay Don't you see? They were the ones who robbed me, the ones who broke into Seekings, the ones who tried to scrobble us just now. We tried to escape them . . . but the Box has brought us right to their lair.

Peter I told you! I don't like all this magic. It gives me indigestion.

Kay But I bet you anything that is where they're keeping Cole prisoner. And Maria. And who knows else.

Peter It doesn't look a very cheery place. We ought to pay attention to those signs.

Kay I don't believe them – as long as we don't talk or make too much noise. Come on.

Kay and Peter edge towards the gate.
An owl cries.

Peter Don't go so fast! Why are you going so fast?

Kay Come on, this is the back way. Look at the ground. No one has been here for weeks.

Peter It gives me the fantods! I don't like this place at all.

They reach the gate.

Kay Well, we're here now. I'm going to climb over and look at the house. Coming?

Peter I'll stay here and . . . keep a lookout . . .

Kay Keep an eye on your watch. It's half-eight. If I'm

not back by nine, take this track down to the village and call for help.

Peter Please don't go! What if they catch you?

Kay Don't worry about me.

Peter I'm not. Oh, and Kay?

Kay Now what?

Peter Can I have the Box, just in case?

Kay Sorry, Peter, better not. Just in case.

He climbs over the gate and disappears.
Birdsong.
Peter left all alone. He starts to doze off. Then he wakes, frightened, in a mist that grows and envelopes him. Then the sound of an aeroplane.

Peter Kay?

Chanting begins, ominous.
Cole Hawlings appears, chained up.

Cole The wolves are running, Master Peter. The wolves are here. Is it safe?

Peter I don't know what you mean –

Maria appears, dirty and bruised. Peter whirls around.

Maria Why haven't you come to rescue me, dear Peter, you plank?

Peter Sister! We're coming . . . Kay's coming.

Caroline Louisa appears, behind bars.

Caroline Peter! Go home. Get away from here. It's not safe!

Peter I'm trying . . . I don't know how.

Now three hooded monks approach him in the mist.

Hello. I think I might be a bit lost.

Charles (*revealing himself*) I think you might be in the soup, ha-ha what!

The monks scrobble Peter, throwing a sack and rope over him.
After they have dragged Peter off, Kay reappears.

Kay Peter? I think I found the place where they're keeping Mr Hawlings and Maria . . . It's the old building by a huge lake . . . I saw that car aeroplane fly in and out . . . Oh no, Peter! . . . Hello! Anyone?

Only wolves growling in the woods.

Hello . . .

The wolves appear, encircling him, appearing for the first time.

I have heard you running a long time. But this is the real attack, isn't it? Those others, in Condicote, those were just warnings.

Nearly upon him now, snarling.

It's all right. I'm ready.

Kay gets out the Box, shaking.
He tries to open it, and the wolves leap on him, roaring as he screams, just vanishing as we go to black.

End of Act One.

Act Two

ONE
TATCHESTER

Bishop and a Carol Choir of five clerics, with Japanese lanterns, singing a medley of carols.

Choir (*jubilant*)
Deck the hall with boughs of holly,
Fa, la, la, la, la, la, la, la, la!
'Tis the season to be jolly,
Fa, la, la, la, la, la, la, la, la!
Fill the mead-cup, drain the barrel,
Fa, la, la, la, la, la, la, la, la!
Troul the ancient Christmas carol,
Fa, la, la, la, la, la, la, la, la!

Deck the hall with boughs of holly,
Fa, la, la, la, la, la, la, la, la!
'Tis the season to be jolly,
Fa, la, la, la, la, la, la, la, la!

They are interrupted by a noisy Paperboy with a pile of the Daily Thriller.

Paperboy Extra! Extra! Read all about it! Mysterious disappearances continue in Condicote! Governess and her children missing!

Choir look a bit dismayed at this, but the Paperboy leaves them to it.

Choir
God rest you merry, Gentlemen,
Let nothing you dismay,
For Jesus Christ our Saviour

Was born upon this Day.
To save poor souls from Satan's power,
Which long time had gone astray.
Oh tidings of comfort and joy.
Comfort and joy
Oh tidings of comfort and joy.

*During the final lines, Charles, disguised under a hat
and scarf, puts a sack over one of the Singers, the
Dean, and scrobbles him.*
    The Paperboy can't wait to return.

Paperboy Mystery deepens! The Merry Dean Disappears!
The Dean of Tatchester Cathedral missing since –
(*Checks watch.*) Teatime!

*The Choir now look around, warily, keeping going
with:*

Choir
While shepherds watched their flocks by night,
All seated on the ground,
The angel of the Lord came down,
And glory shone around –

*Now two more are scrobbled, leaving only three – the
Bishop and two singers. Very uncertain:*

And glory shone around –

Paperboy Another disappearance! Special! Canons of
Tatchester disappear! What clergyman is safe? Murder
gang suspected!

Choir
We three kings of Orient are . . .

Another Cleric scrobbled, just one and the Bishop left.

We *two* kings of Orient are,
Bearing gifts, we traverse afar –

The final Cleric gets done, leaving the Bishop on his own.

Paperboy Now the Cathedral Choir vanishes! European plot suspected! Some fear the Revolution has begun!

The Paperboy stays this time, eyeing the Bishop. Hesitantly, the Bishop begins to sing.

Bishop
Silent night, holy night,
All is calm, all is bright –

Paperboy Stop press! Startling disappearance of the *Bishop* of Tatchester!

The Bishop looks confused at this and, flustered, begins again.

Bishop (*querulous solo*)
Silent night, holy night,
All is calm, all is – aargh!

Finally, the Bishop has been taken too.

Paperboy Stop press! Archbishop of Canterbury offers reward of a thousand pounds for the safe return of the Bishop – or Christmas will be cancelled!

And a sack over his head, he's out too.

TWO
POLICE STATION

We see the Police Inspector, distant and isolated, at a press conference. Cameras flash.

Inspector We of the law will meet this matter with every attention, and although we have no news at the present time, rest assured that we expect developments before too long.

Reporter 1 What are you doing to keep the remaining clergy safe?

Reporter 2 Is it true Christmas may be cancelled?

Reporter 1 And what about the missing children? Any sign of them?

Inspector I invite any persons with information pertaining to the above to telephone Tatchester 7000. Now if you'll excuse me, I need to feed my rabbits.

He gets out a carrot which he feeds cutely to a 'rabbit' under his counter.

THREE
MONK'S PIECE, EARLY MORNING

Pouncer waits for Charles. An assignation. She looks at him in disgust.

Pouncer Really, my darling, must you wear that dog collar everywhere you go? It's becoming rather a habit.

Charles Just playing the part, ha-ha what?

Pouncer Don't you ha-ha what me, my darling. What happened to the dark and dangerous jewel thief I fell in love with?

Charles (*taking off dog collar, a different voice*) He's still very much here, and just as dark and dangerous.

They embrace.

Pouncer I trust you didn't let Abner know you were coming.

Charles No chance. I waited until the old fool had gone for his morning dip in the lake, and then hot-footed it down here. He won't even notice I'm gone. Not with everything else going on.

Pouncer What do you mean? What's happened?

Charles I don't like this, Pounce. Not a bit of it. Scrobbling clergy, women and children. It's not what I signed up to. Why can't we stick to nicking jewels? It won't come to any good.

Pouncer Don't you think I know it? Not for the first time, Abner Brown has promised me treasure – and yet all I get is incessant moaning about this wretched Box of his.

Charles I was turning over the best houses in London. Pearls, diamonds, rubies. More than you've ever dreamed of. I was a guest at the parties of the season. A few cocktails, maybe a dance, slip upstairs while nobody's looking, help myself, and then off again down the drainpipe . . . And now look at me! Scrobbling little nippers. It had better be worth it, Pounce.

Pouncer And have I ever not been worth it, Charlie boy?

Charles No, of course not . . .

Pouncer Have I ever let you down?

Charles I'm not saying that, it's just –

Pouncer I'll tell you what. Why don't you pop that little dog collar back on, and get back to playing vicar, and listen to me. I don't care whether Abner tells you to scrobble the Queen Mother or every last orphan in Britain. Do exactly as he says. Arouse no suspicion. And when the moment is right, when the moment is right, we will strike.

Charles Yes, my darling. Whatever you say. (*Puts on dog collar.*) Ha-ha what?

Beat.

Pouncer Well, what are you waiting for?

Charles Nothing . . . it's just that . . . you know you said you were a . . .

Pouncer A what? A woman who knows herself? Surely not the first one you've ever met, dear Charles?

Charles Yes, but also, that other thing . . . that you were a . . .

Pouncer Spit it out!

Charles A witch! You told me you were a witch. A practiser of the dark arts.

Pouncer I did.

Charles Is that what you're going to do . . . use your magic on him? It's just otherwise, I don't know how we're going to get them jewels, he keeps them under lock and key in his vault –

Pouncer (*grabbing him by the dog collar*) Now you listen to me. There are three things you never ask a witch. You never ask if they *are* a witch, you never ask their age, and you never, ever ask what magic they can do. Do I not look like a witch?

Charles Yes, but . . .

Pouncer Do I not sound like a witch?

Charles Of course, only . . .

Pouncer And do I not act like a witch?

Charles All the time!

Pouncer Then know this. That when I choose to use my magic against Abner Brown, the darkness of midnight itself will be as nothing to the blackness of my spell. There is no demon in the universe strong enough to resist my command. I will call up the sulphurous flames of Hell itself to fry that old sorcerer's wicked bones, and then I will summon every black cat and rotten rat in the land to gnaw them clean until not a scrap remains.

Charles And then we will get our swag?

Pouncer And then we will get our swag! But Charlie boy, who knows what is in this Box of his. I suspect it may be the greatest treasure of all. Now go, my tasty Reverend, and find out what you can. He will never reveal it to me, he fears my powers too much.

Charles Your wish is my command, wicked Witch.

Pouncer Now be gone, before I really lose my temper, and turn you into a toadstool.

Charles Love you, my Pounce.

Pouncer Love you, Charlie boy.

Charles slips away. Pouncer looks after him for a moment, sighing.

Poor, poor Charlie boy. Truly, the only spell I ever cast was convincing you that I was a witch in the first place.

She fades into the night.

FOUR
ABNER'S STUDY

Tiny Kay hides behind a sign:

HOPE-LE-CHESTERS MISSIONARY COLLEGE
CLOSED TO VISITORS UNTIL FURTHER NOTICE

He sees Abner enter his study, and sneaks in behind. There are magical symbols everywhere and a bronze head on a pedestal.

Abner leans down to the Head, who whispers furiously in his ear.

Tiny Kay hides himself away behind a trunk piled high with magical tomes.

Abner surveys some newspapers.

Abner (*browsing*) Ding diddle-ing ding ding ding . . . I see the Duchess has offered seventy thousand pounds for the return of her diamonds! They will not be yours ever again, my dear lady, not even for seventy million . . .

He presses the top of the Head, who makes a buzzing noise.

Send in Charles, will you?

Head Come in, Charles.

Charles enters.

Charles You called, ha-ha what?

Abner I hear you have been criticising my orders.

Charles Who told you that?

Abner So you *have* been undermining my authority, getting all argumentative.

Charles No, I haven't.

Abner See!

Charles It's all this scrobbling . . . kids, Chief! What's it all in aid of? I wish you'd tell me more about this damned Box of yours, ha-ha what?

Abner Tell me, my dear Charles, have you ever heard of Ramon Lully?

Charles You mean the comedian who plays at Wilton's Music Hall? I turned over his dressing room last Christmas.

Abner No, you useless larcenist. *Not* the comedian. I mean the famous medieval philosopher.

Charles I can't say I have, old fruit.

Abner And how about Arnold of Todi, have you heard of him?

Charles Oh yes, Arnold of Todi. He runs that upmarket hair salon in Pimlico. Very *à la mode*.

Abner He does not run a flaming hair salon in Pimlico! He too was a philosopher of the Middle Ages. A *very*, *very* great one. Some might say the greatest . . .

Charles History was always my weak spot.

Abner Let me show you something.

Abner produces a heavy leather tome and shows Charles – and us – an early-modern portrait of a wise old man, who looks oddly familiar . . .

Who do you think this is?

Charles Blow me down with a feather, ha-ha what?! It's that chap we scrobbled, Cole Hawlings!

Abner It does look just like him, doesn't it? But what does the name say below?

Charles R-A-M-O-N . . . Ramon Lully.

Abner Exactly. And when was this book printed my dear Charles? Oh . . . (*Turns to inside cover.*) 1577!

Charles A misprint, ha-ha what?

Abner No, you burglar brain! Don't you see? Cole Hawlings *is* Ramon Lully.

Charles 1577? He's getting on a bit to be touring a Punch and Judy show around the provinces.

Abner May the Devil save me! He has an Elixir of Eternal Life, which is why he is still here, plaguing my every move. Now . . .

He turns to another page, which we also see. This time a more sinister figure, with sharp eyes and a forked beard.

Look at this picture.

Charles What a terrifying devil of a man!

Abner Why, thank you.

Charles Well I never! (*Double-take.*) He looks the very spit of you, chief, the very spit, ha-ha what?

Abner Ye-es. And what does the inscription say?

Charles Arnold . . . of Todi. The hairdresser! (*Sees Abner's face.*) The *philosopher*.

Abner nods.

Golly! You must be hundreds of years old.

Abner Then how did I do it, Charles? How come I'm standing right in front of you here, when I was born in 1487.

Charles You eat a lot of vegetables? Yoga?

Abner The Box, Charles! My Box of Delights.

Charles Of course. (*Beat.*) There's just one thing I don't understand, Chief . . . if you made this jolly Box, then why, er, don't you jolly well have it?

Abner As soon as Ramon set eyes on my invention, he wanted it for himself.

Charles What was he going to do with it?

Abner Oh, something saintly, no doubt. Poor Ramon was trying to use his magical powers to do good. Cure disease. Stop famine. Make dreams come true. The most tiresome kind of magician. And he accused me of wanting to use the Box of Delights to do great harm. The cheek of it!

Charles I know, Chief, I can't think why he thought that, ha-ha what?

Abner Exactly! I wanted to do *unimaginable* harm. I wanted to steal riches, conquer kingdoms and bend entire civilisations to my will.

Charles Everyone needs a hobby.

Abner I travelled backwards and forwards in time. I was all powerful, able to live in the past, the present and the future. I was the greatest villain of every age!

Charles A box that lets you travel through time? Just think of the swag . . .!

Abner Then I arrived in this wondrous century of airplanes, movie theatres and machine guns, only for that wretch Ramon to catch up with me at a fair, and steal my Box using a cheap trick. But I will have it back, I must have it back, by midnight tonight – by Christmas!

Charles Why, is it a present for someone?

Abner No, you laughable lowlife. Because by the laws of magic, if I do not return to my own time by Christmas, I will be stuck here forever.

Charles Steady on, old fruit, it's 1938. That's not such a bad time to be alive, ha-ha what?

Abner But don't you see, you hapless hoodlum? Without my Box, I am nothing. I will be stranded here, and die in obscurity, without even a decent notice in *The Times*!

Charles I see . . . so you're kidnapping bishops and clerics to ensure sure Christmas doesn't happen, which means you can't get trapped here by the laws of magic.

Abner Finally, he sees the light.

Charles sits.

Charles I'm afraid I still don't like it, old man. When this was a simple criminal outfit . . . now, that I can get behind. That's an honest chap's game, that is. But all this magic . . . it gives me shivers, ha-ha what?

Abner You don't believe in magic, do you, Charles?

Charles I can't say I do. Not from Ramon or Cole, whoever he is, or you neither . . . Arnold.

Abner That is very funny.

Charles Why so?

Abner Because magic doesn't believe in you either.

Enter Abner's wolves.

Head No, it doesn't.

Charles No, please, Chief . . .

Abner Steal my Pouncer, would you? My Head never misses a trick. It tells me *everything*.

Charles No! I swear! I never! You're delusional!

Abner Oh, so now you also think I'm delusional, ha-ha what?

A trap opens. Red lights of Hell and the shadows and sounds of an enormous grinding machine.

Charles No, no . . . not – the Scrounger!

Wolves push him in, and Charles disappears in a roar of machinery and mangled cries.

Abner Maybe now, do you believe in magic, Charles? What's that? Take your time . . .

*He laughs cruelly. Tiny Kay, gasps and slips, knocking
a book off.*

Hello! What's that?

*Abner picks up the book, looking around suspiciously.
Kay freezes.*
*Abner opens the door. Pouncer nearly falls in – she
has clearly been listening at the keyhole.*

Pouncer (*covering, shaken*) Abner! My . . . Shield and
Star, do come to breakfast. It's getting cold.

Abner (*not fooled*) For you, my Heaven and Glory, I
would do anything. *Anything.*

*He leaves, taking Pouncer firmly by the arm, while
Kay follows.*

FIVE
ABNER'S CELLS

*Tiny Kay follows Abner to the cells, deep in the caves
below the Missionary College lake, damp and dark,
water running past . . .*

Abner (*offstage*)
Long, long ago . . .

And how is the dear Bishop? Are you ready to tell me
where my Box is yet?

Bishop (*bound and struggling*) I tell you, rascal, I don't
know about any Box! Let me go!

Abner Tell me where my Box is, and I shall! What, you
won't?

He pulls down a chain/handle from above.

You have all had your chance. Your blood will be on your own heads. Tonight, there will be no more choirboys, no more churchmen, no more music. Soon Abner will turn this little tap and let all the water from the lake above down upon your heads. Midnight will strike on the Cathedral clock – and on you all!

He disappears with a flourish of his cape, as Tiny Kay runs to the nearest cell.

Kay Maria!

Maria You took your time. Were you planning to rescue me this Christmas or next?

Kay We haven't got long. What can you tell me?

Maria This gang has scrobbled every single person who works for the Cathedral. They're all locked up down here too.

Kay Yes, the papers are reporting on it now.

Maria Are they full of marvellous headlines about me? 'Wholesale Murder Feared! Shrieks Heard from Shuttered House! Bloodstains in the Snow'?

Kay Er, no . . .

Maria Go on then, what can you tell me?

Kay I spied on Abner. I know why he scrobbled all the vicars – unless he gets the Box back by Christmas, he'll be trapped here forever, and die, a mere mortal.

Maria I'm going to give him a kick in the shins that will be immortal all right.

Kay Is Peter here? I think they grabbed him at the gates.

Maria In the cell next door.

Kay Peter!

Peter Hello, Kay.

Kay Thank goodness you're all right. I was so worried.

Peter It's not so bad really. This cell is more comfortable than my room at school.

Kay I shouldn't have left you.

Peter That's all right. I'm such a plank, aren't I, to let myself get scrobbled like that?

Kay No, Peter, you're not a plank at all. In fact, I think you're very brave.

Maria Brave? The only brave thing he's done is ask for extra gruel at breakfast time.

Peter Thanks anyway, Kay.

Kay And Caroline Louisa?

Maria I've heard her cries. She's down here somewhere, along with all the clergy in the world, it seems.

Peter The Bishop keeps leading them in song. They're determined to make Christmas happen, somehow.

Kay So am I.

Maria And what are you going to do about it?

Peter Yes, Kay, you must get us out of this jam. I don't fancy Christmas cooped up in here. Can your Box get us out?

Kay I don't think it can.

Maria I thought it was overrated.

Kay But perhaps it can take me to someone who can. I don't think I can rescue you on my own, or defeat Abner by myself.

Maria Do you know, I think if anyone could rescue us, it would be you.

Peter For once I agree with my sister.

Kay Do you really? I wish I could be so sure.

Maria But don't you see, silly Kay? Why old Mr Hawlings gave you the Box, and not me, or old Pudding Face next door?

Kay Why?

Maria Because you're a dreamer, Kay. And just maybe that funny old Box might make one or two of them come true.

Kay You truly think so.

Maria I truly think so. As does Peter.

Peter Do I? You bet! Jolly good show, Kay. You'll sort us out, I know it.

Kay In that case, Box, take me swift, to the Police!

He disappears.

Peter I think you're rather sweet on Kay Harker, that's what I think.

Maria Do you want me to poke you in the eye with a stick? I can probably reach through the bars, even from here . . .

SIX
CONDICOTE POLICE STATION

From his lofty perch, the Inspector completes a crossword, making Kay feel even smaller and more insignificant than usual.

Inspector How you do bang on about that Missionary College, Master Kay. This is what is known in medical circles as an h'obsession. How on earth would some young men studying to give their lives to God be able to carry on with all these kidnappings?

Kay With a car that turns into an aeroplane, and back. Like I told you!

Inspector There isn't an aeroplane invented that can do that. Unless you've been reading one of those h'unsuitable paperback novels again . . . the ones set in the future.

Kay But it isn't the future, Inspector. It's now. These men are evil. They are here, in Condicote. And I saw Abner Brown kill someone. Right in front of me.

The phone rings. The Inspector answers.

Inspector Condicote 7000? Yes, sir, speaking . . . Of course, right away.

He hangs up and picks up his truncheon.

Now I'm sorry, Master Kay, you'll have to excuse me. That was the Superintendent. All police leave is cancelled. Every officer in the county is required to protect the Cathedral tonight for their Christmas celebration. It will go ahead! A thousand years. No European revolutionaries will stop us. I hope to see you there. Good day to you.

The Inspector departs briskly as Kay sings to himself.

Kay
And was Tomorrow yesterday?
Or had it been and gone Today?
Will no one say?
I wish someone would say
Long, long ago
Or did Now happen a long time ago?
Long, long ago . . .

93

ABNER'S STUDY

Abner joins in with Kay's chorus, as he slinks on.

Abner The hour grows late! Christmas Eve is upon us, and still no Box. I can no longer trust my mortal accomplices.

He circles his hand over and over in the air over the bronze bust on his desk as he mutters a spell.

O ancient head of long ago . . .
O voice of ages past . . .
All seeing, all powerful . . .
Answer my command!

A wind blows through the study, riffling his magic books.
    A window slams.
    The light changes, as the bronze head twists and stretches into life.

Tell me your news, O magic Head of mine.

Head I am your Head and answer your command!

Abner And what have you seen? Tell me!

Head Your agents have captured every single priest attached to the Cathedral, as well as all the staff.

Abner Is there any chance of their Christmas celebration still taking place?

Head Yes.

Abner Impossible! Tell me then! What are they doing to frustrate me?

Head They are telephoning every church in the country, trying to get replacements.

Abner Then we must stop them! Send some demons to cut all the Tatchester telephone lines and telegraph wires!

The Head shakes, muttering.
    Bat-faced demons explode out of the shadows, scattering to do his bidding.
    The Head sags with exhaustion.

Head It is done.

Abner And will that stop them?

Head No, for friends of the Cathedral are on their way already.

Abner Curse them, and curse you! Dislocate all traffic around Tatchester for twenty miles, so the roads are blocked. Jam the railway points.

Head This is too much magic, even for you, dark lord!

Abner How many times must I repeat myself? Block the traffic, Head, unless you want to stay on that pedestal forever!

The Head shudders with the effort, but mutters a spell.

(*To Head.*) Well?

Head (*exhausted*) They can still come by air.

Abner This cannot happen! Summon a storm.

Head You stretch my powers to the limit.

Abner I made you! Do as I command.

Head (*cold with rage*) Very well. (*Enters spell-casting mode once more.*) Give me a storm from the north, and the east and the south and the west! Flood the countryside with the deepest snow since the wolves first ran! Make the drifts eight feet deep around the Cathedral door!

*Snow begins to spiral out of nowhere, soon rising to
a blizzard which howls and threatens to devour
everything in its path.*
   But producing it has nearly killed the Head too.

Abner So now, everything is done. Tell me, sweet Head –
will I have the Box today?

Head (*weak*) It will be under your hand.

Abner Finally! After centuries, Ramon, Cole, whatever
your name is! Past, present and future, all is mine! I can
open the sluices when I choose, to wash him and all my
prisoners away. Who will bring me the Box?

Head A child. It will come under your hand.

Abner No child or saint can stop me now! To the
strongroom!

*Abner, the Head and the study disappear in the
blizzard of their creation.*

EIGHT
SEEKINGS

*A carol continues as Kay returns with trepidation to
Seekings: bookcases overturned, drawers ransacked –
chaos.*

Kay Hello? Anyone?

*He picks his way through the mess.
   Then he finds his father's painting of Bottler's
Down – slashed.
   He sits down heavily, defeated.
   Gets out the Box, studies it.
   For a moment, he looks like he wants to hurl it at
the wall or out of the window.*

Then he relents, and opens it once more.

Herne! All my friends are captured, and Mr Hawlings too. I am trying to keep you safe but the wolves are running me close. No one else will help. Show me how to bring an end to this.

Herne appears, softer this time.

Herne I know what you want, Kay Harker.

Kay No! No you don't! I am tired of everyone claiming to know what I want all the time! What's for tea, what Maria and Peter want, what I want . . . If you all know so much, why do you need me to get your precious Box and Mr Hawlings out of this mess?

Herne But I do know what you want, Kay. Trust me, I do.

Kay I could go forward in time, couldn't I, with this Box? I could go to Christmas, this year, next year, when we are all together again. Or to any time. Any time would be better.

Herne Is that what you truly want? Time is a big book, with many pages. Who can say if you will find what you are looking for?

Kay Who cares! I want to be done with the whole stupid adventure – even being back at school would be better than this!

Herne Not sure I believe you, Kay. Tell me the time you would like to travel to the most?

Kay I don't know, I . . .

The Box hums. Kay opens it a crack.

No! Why would I do that? I want to forget, don't you see?

Herne Today, Christmas Eve, six years ago.

Kay Don't take me, you can't make me, why would you –

Time-travel music, the Box springs open.
Past Kay appears, reading a book as in the opening scene.

Don't make me live this again, please, Herne! I know it was my fault, I know! I'm sorry!

His Mother and Father appear.

I was only reading a book, that's all. I should have been paying more attention. I didn't notice the log –

A log sparks on to the rug, the fire flares up.
Past Kay steps back, his parents disappear . . .

I can't help it. It's true what they say at school, Caroline Louisa, Maria and Peter. I'm just a wretched dreamer.

He looks up at Herne.

And I let the fire kill my mother and father. Can't I stop it?

Herne The Box allows you to travel through time, Master Kay, but you cannot change it.

Kay Then what is the point? Why did you show me again? Did you think I had forgotten? When I think about that moment every single day?

Herne No, Kay. I wanted you to look. You weren't looking.

Kay What am I looking for?

Herne The truth, Kay.

Time-travel music, as Kay opens the Box again. He is lost in the glowing light, watching the scene again, although this time, only he can see.

Kay Wait, what's that . . . on the roof . . . This I haven't seen before . . . Something in the dark.

Kay slams the Box shut, trembling.

Herne What is it, Kay, what did you see?

Kay Something I can never forgive.

Herne Now you know the true power of this Box. What it will make men do. I am sorry to make you see that.

Kay It's all right, Herne. I am glad I did.

Herne Why?

Kay Because now I know exactly what I have to do. Box, take me swift to Abner Brown!

NINE
ABNER'S VAULT

Tiny Kay appears, following Abner and Pouncer into the vault, where the trunks are piled like strong boxes.
A fire burns in a grate, by a coal scuttle, by a window and a table.
Abner carefully locks the heavy vault behind them.

Pouncer Well?

Abner My Angel of Death, my dear sweet Nightshade, here is what you have been waiting for – you have all been so busy. The poor late Charles, my Pouncer. So terribly busy behind my back.

Abner opens the trunks, pulling out jewels and treasures in turn. He has a jeweller's rag in his pocket, polishing his trophies as he flaunts them to Pouncer.

The dear Duchess's rubies . . . worth thirty thousand if they are a penny . . . These emeralds must be at least

99

twenty . . . And these, my darling, pearls, so light to carry and yet worth so much, fifty thousand for these big ones, I think! And not to mention the sapphires . . . Why, there must be three hundred thousand pounds in here alone.

Pouncer Only because your thieves have worked so hard. Thieves that now want to see their share. Those of us that are still alive.

Abner clutches the jewels to his bosom.

Abner Patience, patience, my jealous Jezebel . . . soon the Box will be mine once more, and then together, you and I will have all the riches and the power in the world.

The floor creaks. Tiny Kay darts under the table.

What's that?

Abner gets out his strangling gloves.

Pouncer Nothing but the wind. I fear all this Box has done is make you paranoid, Abner Brown.

Abner Strange, how just now that boy Kay Harker came into my mind. I failed to kill him once before, but I will not fail a second time.

Abner and Pouncer inspect the room for the noise. While their backs are turned, Kay climbs up the table into one of the trunks.
As he does, the tiny miniaturised Box, in a flash of light, falls out of his pocket on to the floor.

Kay The Box!

Abner (*satisfied*) Very good. Now, er, my Princess of a Pilot, perhaps you might prepare the car-o-plane for our imminent departure.

Pouncer You promise that you will bring my . . . the . . . diamonds directly?

Abner Once I have the Box, and those churchy fools in our cellars have been disposed of, I will bring you the diamonds directly.

Pouncer You swear?

Abner Upon my mother's grave.

Pouncer I thought your mother was a demon.

Abner Precisely. I dare not cross her name, even in death.

Pouncer Very well. But do not be late, oh my mighty master. (*Aside.*) Now is my moment. While he is busy drowning those wretches below, I will take my haul, my sweet revenge – and his precious car-o-plane too.

Abner For you, my Temptress of Time, never. (*Aside.*) My dear, sly, treacherous Pouncer. So, so pretty, but . . . as foolish and weak as her sex are wont to be. She'll never see her share. To make sure of her will be but the work of half an hour!

Back to each other.

Pouncer My Xanadu! I shall see to it that your chariot awaits!

Abner My Kubla Khan!

Pouncer blows him a kiss and leaves.
   Abner packs the cloth and jewels away into the trunk, and closes it, before leaving.
   The Box flashes on the floor.

Kay (*muffled, and banging lid*) Help! Anyone! Help! Let me out!

Just as we think he might suffocate, Pouncer sneaks back in.

Pouncer How right my darling Charles was. What a false-hearted and duplicitous scoundrel is *Abner Brown*.

I have a claim to a good portion of this treasure, being as I stole most of it, yet here it all is, packed up in *his* bags, and ready to go with him in *his* plane. Luckily, he is not as good a thief as I.

Pouncer produces the key she just stole from him. She unlocks the chest Tiny Kay is hiding in, and runs her hands through the jewels in ecstasy.

The Duchess's rubies . . . diamonds, pearls . . . even the special sapphires! Never shall he look upon them again!

Pouncer magics a sack from nowhere and begins to fill it with jewels from the trunk that Kay is hiding in. As she ties the sack up, turning her back, he pokes his head out. She turns back, the sack full and tied.

And that's the lot! Not even one little worthless piece of precious glass shall I leave him.

Kay darts back, drawing Abner's rag over his head.

Wait a moment, though, what's this?

Pouncer picks up the Box of Delights, sparkling.

Nothing. Just an empty jewellery case. Still, might as well add it to the collection!

She pops the Box in her bag.

Now, is there anything else left in here . . .? (*Peering in the trunk.*) Nothing but an old jeweller's rag. From riches to rags. How I wish I could see the old fathead's face when he discovers his loss . . . Wait. I can't leave it empty . . . He will suspect something . . . (*She looks around.*) Ha! Perfect!

Pouncer fills the trunk with coal from the scuttle. We hear Tiny Kay coughing.
Pouncer tries to lift the trunk – checking that it is as heavy as when it was filled with jewels.

Now, swift, the chain – the padlock – (*As she locks it.*)
There, all locked, and no traces left.

Abner (*offstage*)
Long, long ago
Or did Now happen a long time ago?
Long, long ago . . .

Pouncer (*aside*) The treacherous fool returns! I'll distract
him by releasing the prisoners down below.

*Pouncer climbs out through the window, taking the
bag of jewels with her.*

TEN
COLE'S CELL

We see Cole, in his cell, in shadow.

Abner (*offstage*)
Long, long ago
Or did Now happen a long time ago?
Long, long ago . . .

*Dressed for a trip, he enters, dragging the jewellery
trunk in.*

Now Cole, or Ramon, my merry old soul. I have come,
in the spirit of old times, to give you one last chance.
As you see, I am ready to fly. My enemies are in chains,
awaiting a watery fate, Christmas is cancelled, I have my
treasure and my desert island awaits. All I need is my
Box. Where is it?

Cole Nothing you can say, in this time or the next, will
induce me to give that Box back to you. You have shown
yourself unfit . . . Arnold.

Abner You realise the alternative? You see this iron
wheel? It works sluices which will flood these ancient

cellars with twenty feet of water from the lake above. I don't think even your precious Elixir will save you from that.

Cole I will never let any weakness of mine preserve your evil. I would rather die.

Abner Very well then. You leave me with no choice.

He walks to the sluice wheel.

You still refuse? I will have the Box under my hand anyway today. You know the laws of magic, Ramon. My Head told me I would have it, and the Head never lies.

Cole No, the Head never lies.

Abner What do you mean?

Cole The Box shall not be yours, whatever happens to me. And neither shall you have your treasure.

Abner You ramble in your dotage, old man. I have my treasure, just as I shall have the Box under my hand. Look you here.

He opens the jewellery box.
It is full of coal.

I've been betrayed! Very well. I shall have something, though. Revenge! Do you know what this lake above us is famous for?

Cole A very ugly scoundrel living on it.

Abner No, for the fool who drowned like a rat in its waters.

Abner turns the wheel, a groaning noise, a rush of water.
Kay creeps out of the Box, filthy and shaken but alive.

You hear that? The sluice is working beautifully. Thirty feet of water just rushing to drown you all – Clergy, children, Pouncer – the lot of you! And I shall have my Box of Delights! The Head never lies. Farewell Cole, I shan't remember you . . .

Abner blows him a kiss, and departs.

Long, long ago
Or did Now happen a long time ago?
Long, long ago . . .

The water rises.

Kay Mr Hawlings! Mr Hawlings!

Cole (*looking down*) I wouldn't keep that size, if I were you, Master Harker.

Kay I've lost the Box! And now I can't get back to normal.

Cole That's a pity. For the water is a-roaring in and I'm all chained up, as you can see.

Kay Is that it then? Have we lost? Is Abner going to win . . . again?

Cole Come closer, Master Harker, so I can at least see you properly.

Kay does.

The wolves have run us very close, haven't they? But do you remember that time at Seekings, when they got as near . . . and yet I got away?

Kay The painting! But . . .

He looks around.

Cole There is no painting by your father here in this watery cave. You are quite right. But do you have imagination, Kay?

Kay Caroline Louisa says I have too much imagination.

Cole No such thing! And can you draw, like your father?

Kay A bit, but I'm not nearly as good . . . Oh, Mr Hawlings, look, the water, it's coming in!

Cole Then let us hope you are a quick artist. Go to my coat there. If you rummage about in the pockets, what can you find?

Kay rifles through Cole's coat and finds a pencil and notebook – nearly the same size as him. They glow, and the dark cell is illuminated.

Kay A pencil . . . and a notebook. But they are so heavy.

Cole Drag them out, then!

Kay does.

Now, perhaps the wind will settle a little, in favour of a travelling man . . .

Cole blows on his palm, as if blowing something towards Kay . . .
The paper and pencil move by themselves, the pencil circling on the paper.

Now, what can you draw, Master Kay?

Kay I am not very good. I can draw a house, a tree, a train going left to right . . .

Cole What was the last truly beautiful thing you saw?

Kay (*thinks*) I'm not sure . . . I know! My toy boat, the one the Bishop gave me! 'Captain Kidd's Fancy'!

Cole I think that will do us nicely.

Kay drags the pencil . . .
The water rises further.

Do not heed it, Master Kay. Think of your father and mother. How we will avenge them still. Now, what have we drawn?

Kay My boat . . . I think that's the best drawing I've ever done. Can I keep it?

Cole You can do more than keep it. Look what you've done, Kay, you and your imagination.

The paper glows as a life-size version of Captain Kidd's Fancy appears.

Kay But you're still chained up.

Cole Ah yes . . . perhaps you could quickly draw me a key to my chains . . .

Kay sketches, and then chucks a key to Cole.

Kay Quick – we must rescue the others!

Kay and Cole climb in the boat, which begins to sail through the underground tunnels.

ELEVEN
THE RISING WATERS

In smoke and mist, the boat moves across the darkness.
   The water is so loud, as are the screams of the prisoners.
   Peter swims alongside the boat, nearly half drowned.
   Peter shows Kay he has found the Box. It hums. Kay presses it and returns to normal size.
   Then Caroline Louisa climbs on board, hugging Kay and then Peter tight. A moment. Cole looks on fondly.
   Finally, they drag the Bishop up on board.

Kay The Box, Peter, the Box! How did you get it?

Peter That thief Pouncer ran past my cell with a sack of jewels, laughing, so I stuck my foot out and tripped her up.

Kay Bravo, Peter!

Peter She picked herself up and most of the diamonds . . . but left behind this.

Caroline I'll never not believe your stories again, Kay, I'm so sorry.

Kay Your brother was never ill, was he?

Caroline A terrible lie from the people who trapped me here. I went to the station and never got further. A bag over my head, a car that seemed to fly . . . I thought I was done for . . .

Kay It's all right now. We will have Christmas together after all!

Bishop Well done, Kay. Who helped you find us?

Cole No one, Your Grace. He did it on his own using his imagination, that was all.

Bishop What a remarkable young boy. Where are we?

Cole An ancient maze of caves, known only to those who know . . . deep in the heart of the old Chester Hills. But this lake above threatens to drown us all.

Kay What happened to the others, your Grace?

Bishop A woman calling herself Pouncer let them out, only they ran off before reaching me. Thank you, Kay. What time is it?

Kay It's nearly eleven, on Christmas Eve.

Bishop Then we must hurry. The service! How are we going to get out? Our thousandth celebration.

Kay I have no idea.

Maria (*offstage*) Help! Help! Kay!

Kay Maria! We must go back.

The others look at him.

No, you go on. Please. I couldn't bear it if Christmas didn't happen. I'll go back for her.

Caroline Kay, absolutely not. It's far too dangerous.

Kay Box, take me swift to Maria!

He disappears.

Caroline Kay!

She reaches out for him, but the boat sails on.

TWELVE
THE UNDERGROUND RIVER

Kay appears on one side of the bank of the underground river created by the flooding sluice.
  Abner Brown is on the other, holding a struggling Maria tight.

Kay Abner!

Maria He wants to make me walk the plank, but I'm not playing –

She yelps as Abner twists her arm.

Abner I am afraid you are, Miss Maria, whether you care for it or not.

Kay Abner . . . Arnold. Whatever your name is. I came here to tell you something.

Abner Child, there is nothing you can tell me that I do not already know.

Kay (*looking away*) I . . . I . . . I . . .

Abner You want to stutter at me? What?

Maria (*supportive/desperate*) Come on, Kay.

Kay I – I am no longer afraid of you.

Abner Really?

Kay Because I have this.

Kay produces the Box, which hums.

Abner My Box! The Head did not lie, after all. Under the hand of a child, indeed. Its powers are way beyond your juvenile comprehension. Give it to me this instant, or this minx dies a cold and cruel death.

Maria Don't do it, Kay. I'm all right. Well, I can't swim, but apart from that, I'm all right.

Kay You can't swim?!

Maria Look, I can reassemble a pistol in two minutes, but I never said I was perfect!

Kay You didn't need to . . . I'll get you out of this, I swear.

Abner Children! Why do they never learn? I am not joking.

Abner shoves Maria over the edge, with a scream, clutching on with her hands and nails, her legs kicking out over the watery abyss.

Maria I wasn't joking either. For once. I really *can't* swim.

Kay But I have learned something. I have learned that this Box is a beautiful, magical thing. It has shown me – shown us all – the wonders of the world.

Maria It even made me like being a duck! Even though I can't swim. (*To Abner.*) So there! I'm not so scared of you after all!

Kay And I have learned that there is magic in everything, not just in this Box.

Abner You have learned nothing. You are just a little schoolboy, deceived by some old man he met on a train.

Kay The only person who has been deceived is you. You thought you would have the Box under your hand. And you did, earlier, in your vault. But I was so little, you never even noticed.

Abner Give it to me. Now.

He treads on Maria's hands, she screams.

Kay No. Hand over my friend Maria first, then I will give you the Box.

Abner Ha! I was born four hundred and fifty years ago, not yesterday. The delights of the Box are too tempting for anyone who knows them.

Kay Not for me.

Abner What makes you so different?

Kay Because the magic of this Box was once used . . . to do great harm. This Box, this thing of wonder you made . . . also killed my parents.

He holds the Box out over the water.

Abner Lies! You wouldn't dare!

Maria He jolly would. Chuck it, Kay! Don't worry about me!

Kay Herne showed me. You used this to travel to my home. Christmas, six years ago. Your magic Head had told you that a boy called Kay Harker would one day use your Box against you. So, you tried to burn us all to death.

Abner Yes! What of it? They were nothing to me. Now give me the Box, or I shall kill your little friend too. There is no need for anyone else to die, Kay Harker. It is all up to you. Give me my Box of Delights.

Maria Kay, don't be a fool –

Kay looks at the Box, glowing and humming. The most precious and most dangerous thing he has ever owned –
At Maria dangling across the water, just holding on, gasping with effort –
At Abner leaning out for the Box, goggle-eyed, an addict hungering for his fix.

Abner Hurry! Christmas approaches! I will not be trapped here. Now throw me that Box, or I shall send this one tumbling into the waters of eternal sleep.

Maria Don't do it, Kay! I can handle this.

Kay (*quiet*) I'm sorry, Maria. You'll hate me for saying this, but . . . I'm not afraid of you any more either. Because I like you. I . . . *really* like you. And I don't want to lose you. (*Bold.*) I don't want to lose anyone ever again.

With a big, definite swing, Kay lobs the Box over the water to Abner.
It sails through the air, showering light like a comet. Abner catches the Box, triumphant with glee.

Now, let her go!

Abner Very well.

Abner pushes Maria off the edge and she tumbles into the water with a shriek.

Kay Maria!

Kay leaps in after her.
He struggles to catch Maria in the churning torrent.
They turn up and down, gasping for air.

Maria Help – I can't –

Kay I'm know, I'm here –

Down they plunge again, pressing for air against the
sheet of water.
Maria struggles, and begins to go limp.
Above, Abner opens the Box, filling his face with
a demonic light.

Abner (*incantatory*)
Long, long ago!
Or did Now happen a long time ago!
Long, long ago . . . !

Kay is losing Maria, but he has to resurface for air.
We see her turn, unconscious, down into the dark
depths, disappearing.

Kay No!

Kay dives back down after Maria, stretching out.
But it's no good.
She's gone, lost in the murky depths.

Abner
Long ago, long ago, this Box was mine.
Count once, count twice, and thrice
Take me to my own time!

The underground river is filled with an unholy sound.
A helicopter preparing to take off, the whirl and
whoosh of time, a deluge approaching down a tunnel.

Kay (*surfacing*) You murderer! You've killed her!

*Now the light from the Box ripples out over the
cavern, changing, rippling, fading Abner and the Box
in and out of light, as he prepares to disappear into
the past with his prize.*

Abner So I have. Toodle-oo!

*He waves . . . and the car-o-plane zooms up out of the
darkness, above their heads!.*

Pouncer (*voice-over*) Oh Abner, you old rogue, did you
truly think you could diddle Sylvia Pouncer? I have
stolen all your treasure. Every last gem. And this is for
Charles.

*The plane dive-bombs Abner, who yells and tumbles
head first into the underground river with the Box . . .
    Its power is electrified by the current, exploding
with light!
    The old man shudders and writhes, frothing at the
mouth, clawing for air –
    As the water runs deep red with evil.*

Good riddance!

*The car-o-plane sails off to freedom.
    And the sorcerer sinks forever into darkness,
leaving only the Box, bobbing on the surface.
    Emotionally and physically exhausted, Kay can just
reach for it . . .*

Kay Box! Take me swift to Maria!

*Now the water fades away, lifting up, up and up into
the sky.
    Ethereal music as Kay travels under the waves, as
the Box magically brings him to Maria. Her eyes shut,
gently revolving in the beginning of eternal sleep.
    Kay floats towards Maria.
    Still she does not wake.*

He tries to rescue her . . .

But he cannot take her weight and hold the Box at the same time.

The light is fading . . .

Kay lets the Box sink, and grabs Maria.

Her eyes open. They smile, fingers touching, an embrace –

And then he helps her up, as together they move on and out to freedom, sent on their way by one last dying flash of light from the Box of Delights, before it shuts and is once more lost forever in time and space.

THIRTEEN
THE LAKE AT HOPE-LE-CHESTERS

Inspector Halt in the name of the Law! Who goes there!

Bishop The Bishop of Tatchester!

Inspector You are under arrest!

Bishop Whatever on earth for?

Inspector For kidnapping the Bishop of Tatchester, all his clergy, several children and their guardian. *And* the paperboy!

Bishop But I *am* the Bishop of Tatchester!

Inspector shines his torch in the Bishop's face.

Inspector Hmm, I'm afraid I shall have to ask my men to verify your identity down at the station. We are looking for the ringleader of a dangerous band of kidnappers and jewel thieves.

Bishop Then you had better get underground as quick as you can! The villain you're looking for has taken one child hostage and may be about to seriously harm another.

Inspector And how am I to know you are not that villain seeking to make his escape by pretending to be the Bishop of Tatchester?

Maria (*appearing from underground with Kay*) Because the villain is dead! And Kay defeated him!

Peter Maria! You're alive!

He hugs her.

You haven't hurt anyone, have you?

Maria No, this time Kay did all the hurting. He was magnificent!

Kay I think it was Pouncer really . . . And I couldn't have done it without you.

Maria Normally when a boy pays me a compliment, I step on their toe. But for you, Kay Harker, I shall make an exception.

Bishop Yes, well done, Kay! But how did you escape? And what has happened to that villainous rascal

Cole (*mystically*) He has been swept deep into the caves by the flood. I don't think any man will find part of him again.

Maria How do you know?

Cole I know what I was born to know, and what I don't know, I sense. I felt it, Miss Maria, a feeling of great evil leaving the world.

Inspector Nevertheless, I shall have to officially ascertain this. There is another gang member who took off in a plane, which my men said looked like a car, but I blame the snow. They will not get far in this weather. Now, who is responsible for this party here?

Everyone Else Kay Harker!

Inspector A child? A fine tale for Christmas, I must say! I shall interview these gentlemen and get the true story from them tomorrow. Thank goodness the Bishop was there to guide you all to safety.

Kay Inspector! Stop talking and listen to me for once! It's after eleven o'clock on Christmas eve. We must get –

Inspector Trust the Law, Master Kay. The Law never sleeps but sometimes she knows when to close her eyes.

Bishop And now is the time to open your eyes! You must get me, my clergy and these heroic children to Tatchester Cathedral in time for our thousandth Christmas celebration!

Inspector I regret to say that will be quite impossible, Your Grace. You will never get through the snow.

Bishop Then there will be *no* service and *no* Christmas this year in Tatchester.

Cole I would not be so sure, Your Grace. A travelling man can often find a way of doing the impossible, can he not, Kay?

Children He can!

Cole We needn't give up hope yet. Listen . . .

Church bells ringing for the Christmas service in the distance. And then . . . sleigh bells getting louder and louder.

Inspector Why, I do believe it is Father Christmas, children!

Maria Phooey. If Father Christmas ever tries to come down my chimney, I shall light the fire and burn him to a crisp.

Kay It's not Father Christmas though . . .

Herne appears high up, shining and radiant.

Maria Herne! Good-oh! And her sleigh is driven by lions and unicorns, which I far prefer to reindeer, who smell too much of the farm.

Cole Herne, I would keep those lions away from those unicorns, if I were you!

The lions roar their approval.

Herne Get in. Bishop, I can take you all in in this sleigh. Including you, Inspector.

Inspector I thank the lady for her kind offer, but the Law is otherwise occupied, combing these grounds –

Everyone Come on!

They all exit to board the sleigh which we hear depart with bells and roars, and we see a miniature sleigh of people pulled by lions and unicorns fly through the snowswept starry night, singing.

Company (*singing*)
Ding dong, merrily on high,
In heav'n the bells are ringing:
Ding dong, verily the sky
Is riv'n with angel singing.
Gloria, Hosanna in excelsis!

FOURTEEN
TATCHESTER CATHEDRAL

The clock strikes quarter to midnight

Bishop We are back just in time . . . but where are the lights?

Kay Abner Brown used his magic to cut the electricity.

Bishop Quick – everyone, the candles!

Cole and Kay are left alone as Bishop rushes off with the others.

Cole There may be a quicker way. Fetch me that tripod, there, Kay . . . Now here is that bottle which Arnold of Todi wanted nearly as badly as his Box.

Kay Your Elixir of Life?

Cole That very same, which I first discovered in a temple belonging to Alexander the Great. But now its purpose is served. This Feast of Nativity is saved, the Box lost to the waters deep, your parents avenged.

Kay Don't you need it though . . . to live?

Cole I have been on these roads a long time now, Master Harker, through the good times, the bad times and the in-between times. Now I fancy my time is done.

Kay But Cole . . . Ramon . . . Mr Hawlings . . . what if something else bad happens? What if the wolves run again?

Cole Then you will know how to deal with them, won't you?

Kay Without magic, though . . .

Cole It is magic that brought about all this rumpaging, it is magic that set the wolves running in the first place. It is not magic alone you need to beat them, Master Harker, as you have shown. But hope, bravery and love too. Although, I will give you this.

He takes out his bottle of Elixir.

This is the oil that Alexander first found burning in the Geodrasian Wastes, it is the Oil of Eternity. I found it and took it for an Elixir many a year ago, and now my race is run. There is but a drop left. I give it to you, Kay Harker, I give it to you all, and I give it to Christmas!

Cole drops a drop of oil in the tripod.
    A flame shoots up, and everything is illuminated.
    Everyone is there – Caroline Louisa, Peter, Maria, the Bishop, clergy – in a candlelit glow.
    Cole disappears.

(*Offstage.*) May it burn for the rest of time!

The clock strikes twelve.

Kay Thank you, Mr Hawlings! And merry Christmas!

Bishop Merry Christmas *everyone*!

Company
    Good tidings we bring
    To you and your kin;
    Good tidings for Christmas
    And a happy New Year!

    We wish you a merry Christmas
    We wish you a merry Christmas
    We wish you a merry Christmas
    And a happy New Year.

They invite the audience to stand and join in.

    We wish you a merry Christmas
    We wish you a merry Christmas
    We wish you a merry Christmas
    And a happy New Year!

The End.